Horrible Geography

VIOLENT VOLCANOES

AND

EARTH-SHATTERING EARTHQUAKES

Two Horrible Books in One

ANITA GANERI MIKE PHILLIPS

Scholastic Children's Books
Euston House, 71 Euston Road,
London NW1 2RA, UK

a division of Scholastic Ltd
London ~ New York ~ Toronto ~ Sydney ~ Auckland
Mexico City ~ New Delhi ~ Hong Kong

First published in the United States by Scholastic Ltd, 2006
Cover illustration copyright © Mike Phillips, 2002

Violent Volcanoes
First published in the UK by Scholastic Ltd, 1999
Text copyright © Anita Ganeri, 1999
Inside illustrations copyright © Mike Phillips, 1999

Earth-Shattering Earthquakes
First published in the UK by Scholastic Ltd, 2000
Text copyright © Anita Ganeri, 2000
Inside illustrations copyright © Mike Phillips, 2000

10 digit ISBN 0 439 95007 4
13 digit ISBN 978 0439 95007 7

All rights reserved
Printed and bound by Nørhaven Paperback A/S, Denmark

2 4 6 8 10 9 7 5 3 1

The right of Anita Ganeri and Mike Phillips to be identified as the author and illustrator of this work respectively has been asserted by them in accordance with the Copyright, Designs and Patents Act, 1988.

Contents

VIOLENT VOLCANOES

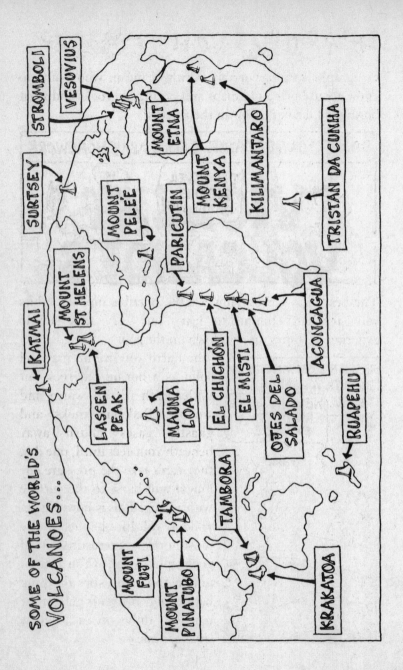

SOME OF THE WORLD'S VOLCANOES...

STROMBOLI
VESUVIUS
MOUNT ETNA
MOUNT KENYA
KILIMANJARO
TRISTAN DA CUNHA
SURTSEY
MOUNT PELÉE
PARICUTIN
KATMAI
MOUNT ST HELENS
ACONCAGUA
LASSEN PEAK
MAUNA LOA
EL CHICHÓN
EL MISTI
OJES DEL SALADO
RUAPEHU
MOUNT FUJI
MOUNT PINATUBO
TAMBORA
KRAKATOA

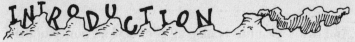

Geography can be horribly boring. I mean, who wants to know about boring old maps and boring old rocks and what boring old farmers grow in their fields?

DON'T FORGET YOUR GEOGRAPHY HOMEWORK

I'LL NEVER GET THIS ON THE BUS!

The best bits of geography are the horrible bits – the bits your teacher's bound to leave out. Try this simple experiment. Jump up and down on the spot.

IT'S AN EXPERIMENT TO DO WITH VOLCANOES, I THINK

WELL, HE LOOKS READY TO EXPLODE

The Earth you live on may feel solid as a boring old rock but underneath it's all warm and wobbly. Red-hot rocks and ghastly gases churn away beneath your feet until, one day, they can't take the pressure any longer and burst to the surface with a bang. This is how you get violent volcanoes, one of the most horribly interesting bits of geography ever. (You might notice the same sort of thing happening with your geography teacher, only on a slightly smaller scale.)

And that's what this book is all about. More powerful than a nuclear bomb, hotter than the hottest oven, more temperamental than your little brother, when a volcano blows its top, it's brilliant, mind-boggling and a red-hot topic, and it certainly isn't boring! In *Violent Volcanoes*, you can...

• watch a volcano erupt (from a safe distance)

• find out why volcanoes smell of rotten eggs
• learn how to spot an active volcano
• train to be a vile volcanologist ...

and, if all else fails, find out which saint to call on if you need saving from a lethal lava flow.

This is geography like never before. And it's horribly exciting.

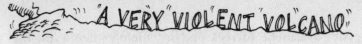

The day a mountain blew apart

It is the morning of 18 May 1980. The dawn is bright and clear over the Cascade Mountains of Washington State, USA. For many months now, the perilous peak of Mount St Helens has been shaken by a series of grumbling earthquakes. Smoke and ash from hundreds of minor explosions have covered the ice-capped mountain in an ugly cloak of black. For weeks, scientists have been monitoring an ominous bulge growing on the volcano's north side – a sure sign that magma deep below the Earth is starting its ground-breaking journey upwards.

As they watch, the bulge keeps growing, relentlessly raising the intense pressure on the gases and magma inside the mountain. Something, surely, will have to give. A dormant volcano, Mt St Helens has not erupted in living memory. Now, after 123 years of silence, this sleeping giant seems to be stirring. To those who watch, it seems almost impossible that this beautiful mountain can be a violent killer. But then, the impossible happens...

At 8.32 a.m., two scientists fly over Mt St Helens. As they approach the summit, all is calm. Seconds later, the mountain shakes with a huge earthquake, dislodging a massive avalanche of rock and ice. Before their eyes, the whole north side of the mountain completely collapses and races downhill at full pelt. Worse is to come. The landslide releases the immense pressure which has been building up inside the mountain. Suddenly, the bulge bursts apart, upwards, outwards and sideways, blasting out a thick, black cloud of hot gas, ash and rock many kilometres into the air. The summit of Mt St Helens is completely shattered.

The scientists have to act fast; the blast cloud is starting to bear down on them. They dive away to the south to safety. The cloud starts expanding to the east, north and north-west, at a speed that could easily overtake their small aircraft. Heading south they are safe for now, but any other direction would mean certain death.

Behind them, the sky turns black as night. Thick showers of ash fall like black rain from the clouds and brilliant bolts of lightning shoot many kilometres into the air. For the next nine hours Mt St Helens continues to erupt, onlookers feel they've had a glimpse of Hell. By evening, the worst explosions are over, but the volcano continues to erupt more gently for four more days. Then at last it falls silent.

One week later, there is another large eruption – several

smaller ones follow, but the main force is spent. Mt St Helens has blown its top. Things will never be the same again.

Ten Earth-shattering facts about Mt St Helens
1 Before the 1980 eruption, Mt St Helens stood 2,950 metres high. The eruption blew an incredible 400 metres off the top which crashed down the mountainside as 8,000 million tonnes of rock. That's a lot of rock.

2 The land around Mt St Helens had been a national park, popular with anglers, campers and walkers. All this changed for ever on 18 May, in the space of just five to ten minutes.

The searing blast cloud, heavy with hot gas, ash and rock, stripped bare the countryside in its path. Instead of thick, green forests and clear blue lakes lay a barren desert of grey ash. The cloud was so powerful that it uprooted every tree for eight kilometres around, picking them up and tossing them aside. As a pilot flying overhead reported, it looked as if:

The cloud was so incredibly hot (between 100 and 300°C) that it boiled the sap inside the trees. Wow!

3 The heat of the blast cloud also melted the glaciers on the summit. Ash and meltwater poured down the mountainside in great, thick rivers of clogging mud. One flowed into the Toutle river, sweeping away people, homes, bridges and hundreds of logs stored at a timber camp. So much mud poured into the Columbia river that it became too shallow for ships to sail and had to stay closed for weeks on end. And the river water became so hot that fish were seen leaping *out* of it!

4 One branch of the awesome avalanche of rocks and ice swept into nearby Spirit Lake, causing waves more than 200 metres high (ten times taller than a house). But most of it raced into the Toutle river at speeds of 100–200 kilometres per hour. It was one of the largest landslides ever recorded.

5 The blast cloud of ash, dust and gas rose 19 kilometres into the air. In two days, it had reached New York. In two weeks, it had travelled right around the world. Ash fell like snow on cities and fields up to 500 kilometres away from the volcano, turning day into night. Airports and roads were closed. In the city of Yakima, 150 kilometres away, the sewage works became clogged with ash and would not work.

6 Mt St Helens began rumbling about two months before its eruption. Warning signs included more than 1,500 small earthquakes which cracked the glaciers on the summit, followed by frequent bursts of steam and ash. Meanwhile, the bulge on its side was growing by two whole metres a day. Everything pointed to a violent eruption. But, when it came, the sheer suddenness and staggering force of the explosion took everyone by surprise.

7 Before the main eruption, hundreds of volcano watchers had come to see the show. Souvenir stalls sprang up everywhere, selling anything from Mt St Helens T-shirts, to mugs, posters and souvenir samples of ash. Even as late as 31 March, a group of people went by helicopter to the summit and began filming a beer commercial! Even today, you can buy glass Christmas tree decorations made from ash from that dreadful day.

8 Scientists set up a seven-kilometre 'red zone' around the mountain to protect people from danger. But it didn't go far enough. Of the 57 people killed that day, all but three were well outside the zone. The dead included campers, sightseers and scientists. One scientist was engulfed by the blast cloud and choked to death as he watched from a ridge nine kilometres away. A worse death toll was only avoided because the volcano blew so early in the day and it was a Sunday.

9 Incredibly, though this was a horribly violent eruption, Mt St Helens seemed to burst apart with barely a sound. The explosion happened so suddenly that the sounds were quickly carried far away.

10 The eruption of Mt St Helens replaced its scenic snow-capped cone with a crater shaped like a horseshoe. But inside the crater, a new dome is growing. Already as tall as an 80-storey building, it will one day fill the mountain and erupt all over again. The burning question is when?

If you compare Mt St Helens to all the eruptions in the history of the Earth, it wasn't even particularly powerful. An eruption five times as big once hit Yellowstone Park, USA. When the rock and ash settled, it covered a third of the USA – but that happened about two million years ago, so you might think it doesn't count.

So, who on Earth came up with the name volcano to describe a smouldering mountain that can explode? Well, there are different stories around the world to explain what causes volcanoes, but you can blame the actual name on the ancient Romans and their hot-tempered fire god, Vulcan...

According to legend, Vulcan lived on the island of Vulcano, inside a smouldering mountain.

SMOULDERING MOUNTAIN

SMOULDERING LOOKS

All the smouldering, sparks and rumbling noises were caused by Vulcan's frantic activities. He was blacksmith to the gods... He made weapons for Mars...

TWANG!

THESE ARE GREAT, I'LL TAKE TWO DOZEN

Armour for Hercules...

HAVE YOU GOT IT IN THE NEXT SIZE UP?

And thunderbolts and lightning for Jupiter.

But Vulcan used his skills in other ways too. For no good reason, Vulcan would pick on villagers and terrorize them with fire, lightning, lava flows and explosions!

So, which came first, Vulcan or Vulcano? No one knows, but the name, tweaked a bit, stuck.

What on Earth are violent volcanoes?

Ask someone to think of a volcano, and they'll most likely describe a neat cone-shaped mountain, gently breathing smoke. But volcanoes aren't always like that. Volcanoes are all horribly different. Some spurt out fire. Others spew out clouds of steam, gas and ash. Some volcanoes explode with a bang, others fizz quietly away. Some are flat or round or lie deep under the sea.

The best you can say is that all volcanoes are built by red-hot magma (liquid rock) from deep inside the Earth. When it bursts or seeps up through a crack in the ground, you know you're dealing with a volcano!

How on Earth do volcanoes happen?

To find out, you'll need one Earth (in good condition), with a large-ish chunk cut out. The Earth looks rock solid, feels rock solid and in many places it is rock solid. But not all the way down. The Earth's made of layers, a bit like a big – a really, really big – onion.

You can't see these layers (even your know-all geography teacher can't see them), but these pictures might give you an idea of what they're like.

EARTH: THE INSIDE STORY

LAYER 1: THE CRUST

THAT'S THE BIT YOU'VE BEEN JUMPING UP AND DOWN ON. JUST LIKE THE CRUST ON A LOAF OF BREAD, IT'S THE EARTH'S OUTERMOST LAYER. MADE OF HORRIBLY HARD ROCK. ON LAND, IT'S COVERED WITH SOIL, GRASS, COWS, YOU NAME IT. UNDER THE SEA, IT'S COVERED WITH, WELL, SEA. IT'S PATHETICALLY THIN (GEOGRAPHICALLY SPEAKING) – ABOUT 40 KM ON LAND, AND A MERE 6-10 KM ON THE SEABED (BUT IT'S VERY STRONG, SO YOU WON'T FALL THROUGH).

LAYER 2: THE MANTLE

THE NEXT LAYER DOWN IS CALLED THE MANTLE. HERE THE ROCKS GET SO VIOLENTLY HOT THEY'VE PARTIALLY MELTED INTO LIQUID ROCK, CALLED MAGMA. IT'S THICK AND GOOEY, LIKE STICKY TREACLE AND SIMMERS AWAY AT A SCORCHING 1980°C. THAT'S HOT, WHEN YOU THINK THAT A KETTLE BOILS AT 100°C, AND THE HOTTEST TEMPERATURE INSIDE A COOKER IS 250°C. THE MIGHTY MANTLE'S ABOUT 2,900 KM THICK – AND HAS NOTHING TO DO WITH THE MANTELPIECE OVER YOUR FIREPLACE.

IS IT ME, OR IS IT HOT IN HERE?

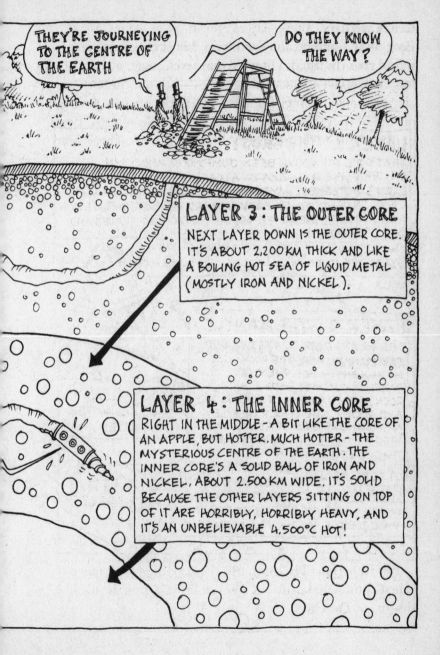

THEY'RE JOURNEYING TO THE CENTRE OF THE EARTH

DO THEY KNOW THE WAY?

LAYER 3: THE OUTER CORE

NEXT LAYER DOWN IS THE OUTER CORE. IT'S ABOUT 2,200 KM THICK AND LIKE A BOILING HOT SEA OF LIQUID METAL (MOSTLY IRON AND NICKEL).

LAYER 4: THE INNER CORE

RIGHT IN THE MIDDLE - A BIT LIKE THE CORE OF AN APPLE, BUT HOTTER, MUCH HOTTER - THE MYSTERIOUS CENTRE OF THE EARTH. THE INNER CORE'S A SOLID BALL OF IRON AND NICKEL, ABOUT 2,500 KM WIDE. IT'S SOLID BECAUSE THE OTHER LAYERS SITTING ON TOP OF IT ARE HORRIBLY, HORRIBLY HEAVY, AND IT'S AN UNBELIEVABLE 4,500°C HOT!

Cracking up

Back on the surface, the Earth's creaking crust isn't a single slab of rock. In fact, it's cracked into seven enormous (and 12 less enormous) chunks, called plates – but not the sort you eat your school dinner from. It's like a sort of crazy paving, on an unbelievably massive scale. The chunks of crust float or drift about on the magma in the mantle below. This is how it happens:

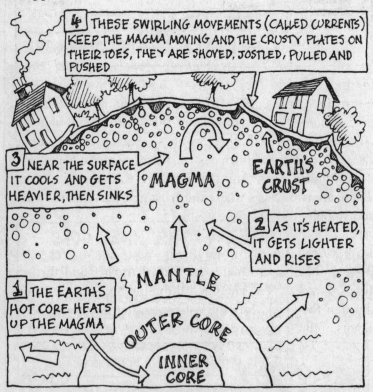

4 THESE SWIRLING MOVEMENTS (CALLED CURRENTS) KEEP THE MAGMA MOVING AND THE CRUSTY PLATES ON THEIR TOES, THEY ARE SHOVED, JOSTLED, PULLED AND PUSHED

3 NEAR THE SURFACE IT COOLS AND GETS HEAVIER, THEN SINKS

MAGMA

EARTH'S CRUST

2 AS IT'S HEATED, IT GETS LIGHTER AND RISES

1 THE EARTH'S HOT CORE HEATS UP THE MAGMA

MANTLE

OUTER CORE

INNER CORE

PS To be horribly technical, the way the plates move is called continental drift but you can leave boring details like this to your teacher.

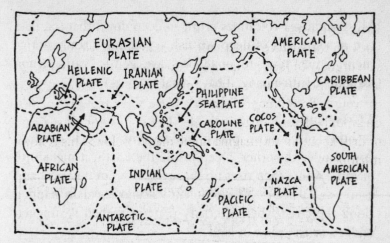

Danger zones

Normally, continental drift just drifts along without you ever noticing. But eventually all this pushing and shoving takes its toll. After all, there's only so much pressure a plate can take. The crumbling crust at the edges of the plates gets weaker and weaker. And this is where volcanoes are born. There are two places where the crust gets particularly weak and wobbly.

1 *Spreading sea floor*

In some places, two plates are pulled further and further apart. Until ... CRAAACK! Bubbling magma wells up through the crack, hits the cold sea water and forms long chains of underwater volcanoes.

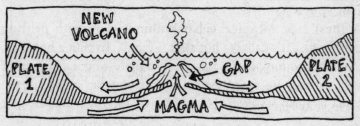

Most undersea volcanoes erupt so deep down that – unless you're some sort of deep-sea fish – you don't really notice them. They tend to ooze out lava gently, rather than exploding with a bang. That's nice!

2 *Going under*

In other places, two plates collide. One plate is dragged down under the other. Deep inside the Earth, it melts into magma, which then rises up through cracks in the crust and erupts as a volcano. These violent volcanoes usually happen along the coast where a crusty plate of seabed is dragged under a crusty plate of land.

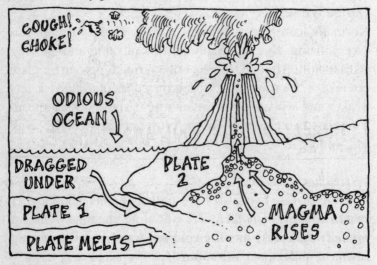

Hot spots

A third type of volcano has nothing to do with drifting continents. It's called a hot spot volcano. To spot a hot spot, you need to look at the middle of a plate where a stream of magma rises up from the mantle. It punches a hole in the crust to form a volcano. Over billions of years, the hot spot stays still but the plate above it crawls slowly over it. As it does so, the old volcanoes die but new holes are punched to make new volcanoes. Slowly, really, really slowly, over millions and millions of years, a chain of volcanoes builds up. This is how the volcanic islands of exotic Hawaii in the Pacific Ocean came into being.

PEACE AND QUIET ABOVE...BUT BELOW...

MAGMA

...HUBBLE, BUBBLE, BOIL AND TROUBLE!

Earth-shattering fact
And if violent Earth volcanoes weren't enough, what about volcanoes in outer space? Most of these are long dead ... but not all. At the last count there were 1,728 active volcanoes on violent planet Venus (precisely 228 more than on Earth) and even more on Io, one of Jupiter's moons. They spit out plumes of stinking sulphur gas up to 300 kilometres high. Which is pretty good spitting by anyone's standards.

Sleeping beauties

But don't be fooled. One thing to remember about volcanoes is that you can't trust them. Not an inch. Volcanoes are horribly unpredictable.

Officially, volcanoes go through three phases. Though not necessarily in this order. These are:

1 Active – a volcano that is erupting now or has erupted in the past. Some volcanoes are more active than others. Some erupt almost all the time. DON'T PANIC! The last volcano in the UK stopped being active about 50 million years ago. Even teachers can't remember that far back.

2 Dormant – a volcano that isn't erupting now but probably will in the future. Dormant means asleep. That doesn't mean it's not dangerous. A dormant volcano can sleep peacefully for weeks, months and even centuries on end, then suddenly wake up. And generally speaking, the longer it snoozes, the bigger the bang next time.

3 Extinct – a volcano that has stopped erupting and isn't likely to erupt again. A dead volcano. Probably. Even dead, a volcano's dangerous. Take Tristan da Cunha, for example, a volcanic island in the South Atlantic Ocean. Everyone thought it was long extinct, until one day in October 1961, when Tristan da Cunha suddenly blew its top. To escape, the 280 islanders took to the sea in their boats. It was two long years before they were allowed home again.

WHAT D'YOU MEAN, I ROW FOR THE FIRST TWO YEARS THEN IT'S YOUR TURN?

Violent Volcanic facts to test your teacher

How many violent volcanoes are there on Earth? How big is the biggest ever? Where do most volcanoes erupt? Try this quick-fire quiz to find out.

1 There are about 1,500 active volcanoes on Earth. TRUE/FALSE?

2 Most volcanoes erupt at sea. TRUE/FALSE?

3 Tristan da Cunha is the most active volcano on Earth. TRUE/FALSE?

4 The largest active volcano on Earth is Mt Everest. TRUE/FALSE?

5 The biggest volcano in the known universe is Olympus Mons on Mars. TRUE/FALSE?

6 The 1980 eruption of Mt St Helens was the deadliest ever known. TRUE/FALSE?

7 In 1883, Krakatoa in Indonesia exploded with the loudest sound ever heard. TRUE/FALSE?

8 Volcanoes can be as violent as a nuclear bomb. They produce the same amount of energy. TRUE/FALSE?

9 If you want to see a volcano, head for Indonesia. It's the most violently volcanic place on Earth. TRUE/FALSE?

10 All volcanoes are millions of years old. TRUE/FALSE?

Answers:

1 TRUE. And about 50 of them erupt every year. More than half lie clustered in the "Ring of Fire" which circles the Pacific Ocean. Here the sea floor is being dragged under the land.

2 TRUE. Only about a third of all active volcanoes bubble away on land. The rest are hidden underwater, along with a million others which are dormant or extinct. Sometimes underwater volcanoes grow so tall, their heads poke up above the waves and form islands.

3 FALSE. Kilauea, Hawaii, is much more active than that. It has erupted non-stop since 1983 and has several craters, not just one. The one that started erupting in 1983 is called Pu'u O'o. Since the eruptions started the island of Hawaii has gained an extra 1.5 square kilometres of new land – that's about the same as 140 football pitches.

4 FALSE. The record-holder is Mauna Loa in Hawaii. It measures 120 kilometres across and stands 9,000 metres from the ocean floor as an awesome island. Mt Everest only stands 8,848 metres tall. And it isn't even a volcano.

5 TRUE. Olympus Mons stands 27 kilometres high, three times taller than Mauna Loa (see above), and is an

26

incredible 650 kilometres in diameter. At the top is a crater as big as a city. This voluminous volcano last erupted about 200 million years ago and is now extinct – luckily for any Martians.

DINNER WILL BE LATE, THE VOLCANO'S GONE OUT AGAIN!

6 FALSE. The worst eruption of recent times was that of Tambora, Indonesia in 1815. It threw out more than 100 cubic kilometres of ash, lowering the island more than a kilometre. 92,000 people died. This eruption was 100 times more violent than that of Mt St Helens.

7 TRUE. This amazing explosion was heard in Australia, a staggering 4,800 kilometres away. Ear-witnesses said it sounded like heavy gunfire. And the shock was felt 14,500 kilometres away in California, USA.

8 FALSE. The energy produced by Mt St Helens in 1980 was equal to 2,500 nuclear bombs, not one. Truly awesome energy.

9 TRUE. Indonesia has more than its fair share of active volcanoes, about 125 in all. That's because it lies on the edges of several different plates of crust and in the Ring of Fire. Runner-up is Japan, with the USA in third place.

10 FALSE. It's true that some volcanoes are horribly old (at a million years old a volcano is still in its prime), but there are some real youngsters around. The youngest volcano on land is Paricutin in Mexico which erupted in 1943. A mere baby in volcanic terms. Amazingly, a Mexican farmer witnessed Paricutin's birth. Now there's something you don't see every day. This is what happened...

The terrified farmer leaps on his horse and gallops for cover

FASTER!

THAT EVENING

The crack has grown into a large hole, red-hot rocks, ash and cinders shoot into the air, flashes of lightning streak across the sky. Every few seconds the ground shakes.

NEXT DAY

BY THE END OF THE WEEK

Overnight the volcano erupts non-stop and it's cone grows 50m high. And it's still growing, hour by hour...

The cone now stands at 150m high. It erupts violently, shooting balls of fire high into the sky. Farmer Dionisio packs his bags as lava destroys his village

EIGHT MONTHS LATER...

Paricutin's cone now stands 270m high. It lives up to its name, El Monstre, the Monster. Smaller monsters appear on its sides.

NINE YEARS AND 42 DAYS LATER...

Paricutin stops erupting, as suddenly as it began. It now stands 450m high. It has buried several more villages, hundreds of homes and covered farms with thick ash. Nothing can grow here now.

TODAY... A large, black glowering hill marks the spot where peaky Paricutin was born. Villages and homes are rebuilt, at a safe distance. For the time being, Paricutin sleeps peacefully... but for how long? No one knows...

Paricutin gave geographers a brilliant opportunity to study a violent volcano firsthand. But volcanoes still remain horribly mysterious. And horribly difficult to predict. So what exactly is it that makes a volcano tick?

While you're sneaking a snooze in your geography lesson, or vegging out in front of the telly, spare a thought for the poor old Earth. Beneath your feet, the energetic Earth never gets a moment's rest. It's always on the go. And it's this earthly activity that causes volcanoes. The burning question is how?

How on Earth do volcanoes erupt?

1 Deep underground in the mantle, magma rises upwards. It rises because it's mixed with gas so it's lighter than the rocks around it. To see how magma rises, try this edible experiment:

What you will need:
- two corks (for the magma)
- a jar of honey (for the rocks)

What you do:

a) Push the corks into the honey so they are completely covered.

b) Watch them bob upwards. Just like magma (well, almost).

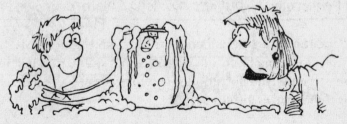

31

c) Spread the honey on toast and eat it. (Take the corks out first.)

2 The magma rises into the crust. As it squeezes and pushes its way up, the pressure mounts. The gases inside it bubble and fizz (like a can of pop if you shake it). The pressure goes up...

CRUST (THE EARTH'S, NOT THE TOAST'S!)

3 And up ... and up.

4 ... until, one day, the magma and gas rush upwards, burst out through cracks in the crust, and erupt. (As the pop will when you open the can, so be warned.)

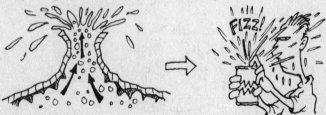

FIZZ!

5 Above the ground, magma's called lava. It's red-hot, sticky and in a hurry. It bursts out with a bang or oozes out steadily, building a cone or creeping across the ground. Eventually, it cools and becomes solid cold rock.

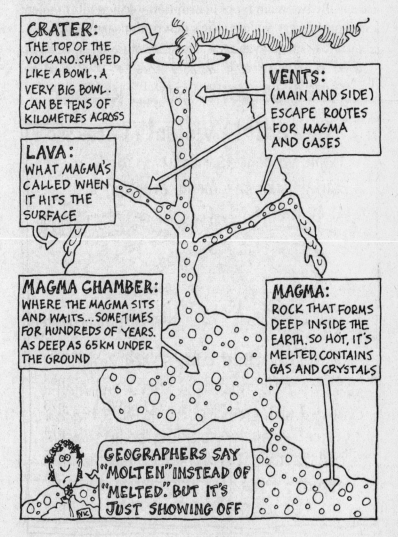

CRATER: THE TOP OF THE VOLCANO. SHAPED LIKE A BOWL, A VERY BIG BOWL. CAN BE TENS OF KILOMETRES ACROSS

VENTS: (MAIN AND SIDE) ESCAPE ROUTES FOR MAGMA AND GASES

LAVA: WHAT MAGMA'S CALLED WHEN IT HITS THE SURFACE

MAGMA CHAMBER: WHERE THE MAGMA SITS AND WAITS... SOMETIMES FOR HUNDREDS OF YEARS. AS DEEP AS 65KM UNDER THE GROUND

MAGMA: ROCK THAT FORMS DEEP INSIDE THE EARTH. SO HOT, IT'S MELTED. CONTAINS GAS AND CRYSTALS

GEOGRAPHERS SAY "MOLTEN" INSTEAD OF "MELTED". BUT IT'S JUST SHOWING OFF

All shapes and sizes

Needless to say, not all volcanoes are shaped like this. It all depends on exactly what type of magma they're made from (thick or thin) and exactly how violently they erupt. There are usually two main types of eruption – **1** incredibly violent and **2** not so very violent (Vic's descriptions, not official).

TYPES OF VOLCANO—REPORT

① **Incredibly Violent** (IV, for short)

Some volcanoes really go with a Bang! Like the mega-eruption of Mt St Helens.

The Magma that causes very violent Volcanoes is thick and sticky, and highly charged with gas. It bursts to the surface in a violent explosion, blasting boiling-hot clouds of rock, ash and gases into the sky.

Verdict: Dreadful, destructive and dangerous to Know.

2) Not very violent (NVV, for short)

If magma is thin and runny, gases escape from it easily, so any eruption is much less violent.

Lava oozes gently from the ground, and flows away in streams. And it can flow for miles, burning and burying everything in its path. They also produce fabulous firework displays, spraying sparkling fountains of lava high into the air.

Verdict: silent-ish, but deadly.

Of course, there are always exceptions to every rule. Some volcanoes start off life as one type and end up as another. Some erupt in both ways at the same time. Phew!

Earth-shattering fact
All that huffing and blowing takes its toll so some volcanoes sneak a short rest between eruptions. Stromboli in Italy erupts quite gently most of the time. In between each small eruption, it only has a 15–20 minute breather – so it could be erupting as you read this fact. El Chichon in Mexico takes a bit longer. It slumbers away for about 1,000 years between eruptions. Just to keep you guessing.

Spotter's guide to volcanoes

Can't tell your shields from your cones? Getting your magmas in a muddle? Help is at hand! With this sizzling new spotter's guide, your worries will soon be over.

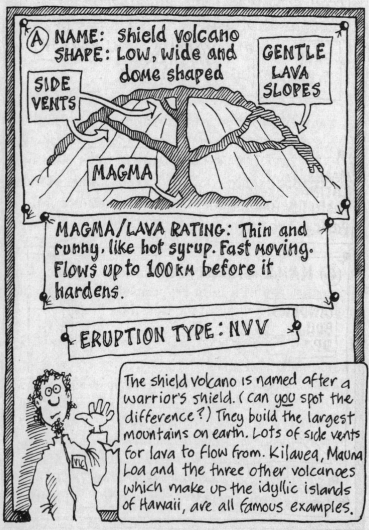

(A) **NAME:** Shield volcano
SHAPE: Low, wide and dome shaped

GENTLE LAVA SLOPES

SIDE VENTS

MAGMA

MAGMA/LAVA RATING: Thin and runny, like hot syrup. Fast moving. Flows up to 100 km before it hardens.

ERUPTION TYPE: NVV

The shield volcano is named after a warrior's shield. (Can you spot the difference?) They build the largest mountains on earth. Lots of side vents for lava to flow from. Kilauea, Mauna Loa and the three other volcanoes which make up the idyllic islands of Hawaii, are all famous examples.

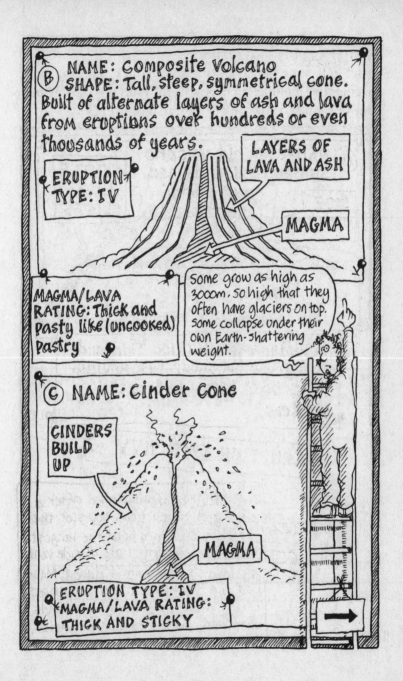

NAME: Composite Volcano
SHAPE: Tall, steep, symmetrical cone. Built of alternate layers of ash and lava from eruptions over hundreds or even thousands of years.

ERUPTION TYPE: IV

LAYERS OF LAVA AND ASH

MAGMA

MAGMA/LAVA RATING: Thick and pasty like (uncooked) pastry

Some grow as high as 3000m, so high that they often have glaciers on top. Some collapse under their own Earth-shattering weight.

NAME: Cinder Cone

CINDERS BUILD UP

MAGMA

ERUPTION TYPE: IV
MAGMA/LAVA RATING: THICK AND STICKY

37

A (truly) bad day in Pompeii

Well, they're not talking about their pizzas. What else would you expect three volcanologists to discuss over dinner? Yup, they're talking about types of volcano. This is where the names come from:

- Strombolian after the Stromboli volcano in Italy.
- Hawaiian after the Hawaiian volcanoes (which is horribly misleading since Iceland's volcanoes are also Hawaiian!).
- Plinian, after Pliny the Elder. He was a Roman nobleman and writer (with a special interest in geography!) who died when Mt Vesuvius erupted in AD 79 and buried the town of Pompeii in ash.

Plinian volcanoes are the most violent volcanoes of all. Luckily (for us), the eruption was witnessed first-hand (though from a safe distance) by Pliny's 18-year-old nephew, Pliny the Younger. He wrote about the dramatic events in a letter to a friend. It was the first-ever eyewitness account of a violent volcanic eruption. Here's a very, *very* rough translation!

Naples, Italy
AD 79

Dear Tacitus,

I'm sorry I haven't written for ages. Thanks very much for the history books you sent for my birthday. I'm just finishing 'A Beginner's Guide to Gladiators', then I'll start yours. Things have been pretty grim since I wrote to you last, what with Mount Vesuvius erupting and everything. You probably heard all about it in the news but Mum and I were actually there!

We were staying with Uncle Pliny in 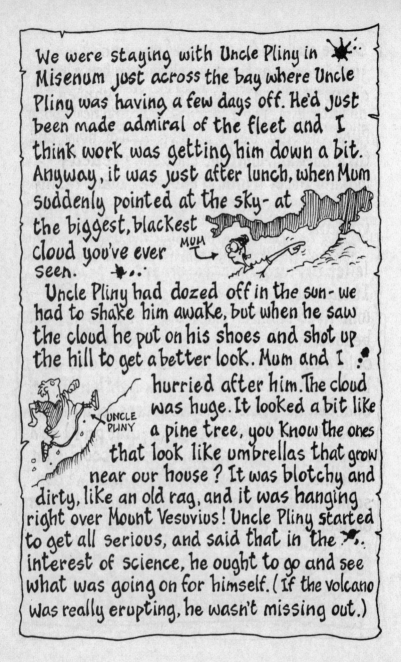 Misenum just across the bay where Uncle Pliny was having a few days off. He'd just been made admiral of the fleet and I think work was getting him down a bit. Anyway, it was just after lunch, when Mum suddenly pointed at the sky- at the biggest, blackest cloud you've ever seen.

MUM

Uncle Pliny had dozed off in the sun- we had to shake him awake, but when he saw the cloud he put on his shoes and shot up the hill to get a better look. Mum and I hurried after him. The cloud was huge. It looked a bit like a pine tree, you know the ones that look like umbrellas that grow near our house? It was blotchy and dirty, like an old rag, and it was hanging right over Mount Vesuvius! Uncle Pliny started to get all serious, and said that in the interest of science, he ought to go and see what was going on for himself. (If the volcano was really erupting, he wasn't missing out.)

UNCLE PLINY

So he called for a boat (you can if you've just been made an admiral) to take him across the bay. He asked me if I wanted to go with him. "You'll learn something new, young Pliny," he said. But I said I'd stay at home, and take care of Mum (not that she needed looking after - funnily enough, I didn't really fancy coming face-to-face with an erupting volcano.)

Just as Uncle was leaving, a letter arrived, marked urgent. It was from his friend, Rectina, who lived right on the slopes of Vesuvius. She begged my Uncle to come and rescue her. The only way to escape from her house was by boat. So Uncle Pliny, always a gentleman, changed his plans and gave orders for a warship to be launched (yet another admiral's perk). He'd save Rectina and anyone else he could find.

Well, we never saw Uncle Pliny again. We heard, some time later, that he'd sailed straight into the danger zone (he always was a bit of a show off)

while everyone was running away. And by the time he got there, thick, hot ash was falling from the sky, followed by great lumps of pumice and rock. Most people would have run for their lives, but Uncle Pliny was there in the interest of science, so he started taking notes. (Well, he didn't actually write them himself. He was far too busy giving orders. No, he had a scribe do all his writing - poor bloke probably wished he'd never learnt to write.)

Anyway, to cut a long story short, it was too dangerous to land near Rectina's house, so the ship sailed to nearby Stabiae, where 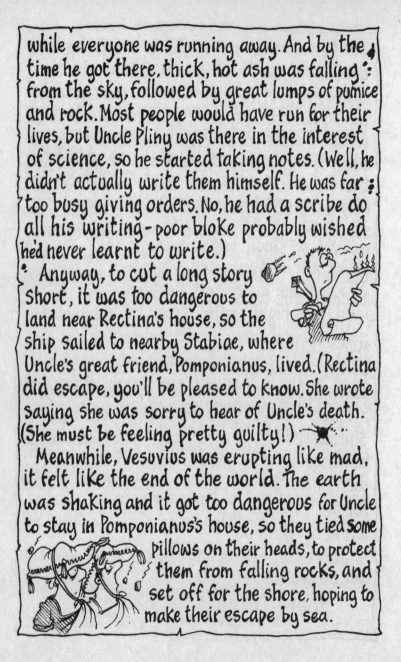 Uncle's great friend, Pomponianus, lived. (Rectina did escape, you'll be pleased to know. She wrote saying she was sorry to hear of Uncle's death. (She must be feeling pretty guilty!)

Meanwhile, Vesuvius was erupting like mad, it felt like the end of the world. The earth was shaking and it got too dangerous for Uncle to stay in Pomponianus's house, so they tied some pillows on their heads, to protect them from falling rocks, and set off for the shore, hoping to make their escape by sea.

But the sea was too choppy to launch the boat.
Even Uncle must have been frightened but he
didn't let on (he never liked to worry others).
He lay down to rest and, someone said, he kept
asking a slave for a drink of water.
Soon they could smell burning,
there was a fire nearby, and it
was getting closer. Uncle Pliny
struggled to his feet and tried to walk away.
But he couldn't make it. Suddenly, he collapsed
and fell to the ground. He couldn't breathe
because the fumes were so thick.

They found Uncle's body two days later. The
man who found him said he looked like someone
asleep rather than someone who had just
died, so hopefully he didn't suffer too much.

Mum's been very brave about it but I know
she misses Uncle very much. So do I, even though
he always found a reason to tell me off. At least he
died a hero. Others died too. Have you heard about
Pompeii? We saw it last week. There's nothing
left at all. Nothing!

Sorry this letter's been so gloomy. Come and
see us soon.

Yours Pliny

Five fiery facts about Pompeii

1 In the first century AD, Pompeii was a large, well-off Roman town near Naples, Italy. Twenty thousand people lived there. The poet, Florus, described it as...

2 Mt Vesuvius had been dormant for 800 years and most people thought it was extinct. No one dreamt it would suddenly wake up. Many people didn't even know it was a volcano.

3 The eruption began at 10 a.m. on 24 August AD 79. Within a few short hours, Pompeii had been buried under several metres of hot ash and rock, leaving no trace of the town.

4 At least 2,000 people died on that fateful day, most of suffocation. Ten slaves died together, crossing a roof. A band of gladiators perished in a tavern. Hundreds of people were trapped in the ruins of their homes. Many more fled for their lives. Those who died were caught by two huge blasts of ash and gas that rolled relentlessly down the mountainside. It must have been terrifying.

5 Geographers use the word Plinian to describe volcanoes which erupt like Vesuvius. Their especially violent features include an enormous blast of gas lasting from a few hours to several days, which shoots out huge amounts of rock and ash. This eventually falls, like a sinister, suffocating snowstorm.

Violent and deadly

Devastating and deadly though it was, in the top ten worst ever violent volcanoes, Vesuvius hardly rates as violent at all. In geographical time (which is much, much longer than normal time. Is that why geography lessons seem to last so long?), Mt Vesuvius wasn't even that bad. To get an idea of exactly how violent a volcano is, scientists use the Volcanic Explosivity Index (VEI, for short), with grades from 0 (gentle) to 8 (cataclysmic). The biggest recent eruption was Tambora, Indonesia, in 1815. It scored a 7 on the scale. (Incredibly, Mt St Helens only scored 5.) The modern world has never experienced a VEI 8 eruption.

Check out the chart on page 46 for the terrifying top ten of the world's most violent eruptions over the last seven thousand years. In order of age, they are:

VOLCANO/LOCATION	DATE	VEI
10: Crater Lake, Oregon, USA	c.4895 BC	7
9: Kikai, Japan	c.4350 BC	7
8: Thera, Greece	c.1390 BC	6
7: Taupo, New Zealand	c.130	7
6: Ilopango, El Salvador	c.260	6
5: Oraefajokull, Iceland	1362	6
4: Long Island, New Guinea	c.1660	6
3: Tambora, Indonesia	1815	7
2: Krakatoa, Indonesia	1883	6
1: Novarupta, Alaska	1912	6

Earth-shattering fact
The last VEI 8 eruption was Toba, Sumatra, 75,000 years ago. This gigantic explosion pumped so much ash and gas into the atmosphere that it completely blocked out the Sun. Temperatures plummeted and the Earth was gripped by a freezing volcanic winter which lasted for years and years. DON'T PANIC! Really violent eruptions are much rarer than smaller ones because it takes much longer to build up the pressure needed to make a really big bang.

Awesome ash ratings

Another way of estimating the Earth-shattering size of an eruption is to measure the amount of ash belched out. (Be warned, this could take some time!) For example, temperamental old Toba (with its VEI score of 8) threw up 2,800 cubic kilometres of ash. That's a thousand times more than Mt St Helens which produced a pathetic 2.5 cubic kilometres. Chart-topping Novarupta, number one for the 87th year running (with a VEI score of 6), blasted out 21 cubic kilometres of ash, equal to about eight Mt St Helens. And if you bear in mind that it only takes one paltry cubic kilometres of ash to fill *half a million* Olympic-sized swimming-pools, we're talking awesome amounts of ash.

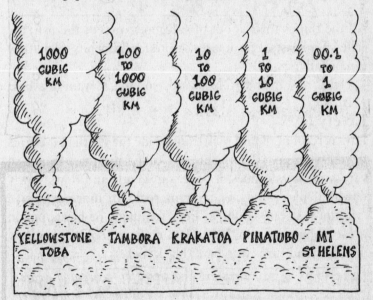

But awesome ash isn't the only thing that comes out of violent volcanoes. They've got a whole range of sinister surprises churning away in their red-hot insides.

The most horribly dangerous thing about volcanoes is not what goes in but what comes out. There's lava, of course, and lots more besides. Red-hot rocks the size of cars, murky mudflows, smouldering showers of ash and cinders, even fish. That's right, fish!

All the things thrown out of volcanoes (except the fish) are called pyroclasts, a posh Greek word for 'fiery bits'. And they can be killers.

Here are some horrible hazards you might want to avoid:

Lively lava

Lava is red-hot, liquid rock from inside the Earth that erupts from a volcano. (Before this, it's called magma.) In not-so very-violent volcanoes, it oozes out gently and flows slowly downhill like a red-hot river of rock. In more explosive eruptions, it bursts out in fiery fountains or blasts out in great globules of goo. When lava cools, it looks completely different and turns into hard, black rock.

Ten flaming facts about lava

1 Liquid lava is hair-raisingly hot. It's never cooler than 800°C and can reach a sizzling 1200°C. That's 12 times hotter than boiling water. A scientist who (unwisely) walked on top of a lava flow still had smoking socks when he took his boots off several hours later!

2 Lava rarely flows faster than a few kilometres an hour so there's normally time to escape. But speed isn't everything. Once lava gets going, nothing can stop it. It grinds along, like a gigantic bulldozer, burying roads, cars, even whole villages, and setting fire to houses and trees.

NOW, WHERE DID I PARK THE CAR?

3 The fastest-ever lava flow leaked out of a lake on Nyirangongo volcano in Zaire in 1977. Racing along at over 100 kilometres an hour, it caught local people by surprise. Tragically, hundreds were killed.

4 If you can't beat the lava, get out of its way. When a lava flow threatened the town of Kalapana in Hawaii in 1983, people took drastic action. They hoisted their houses (and local church) on to the back of lorries and moved them away to safety. Behind them, the town burned to the ground.

5 The longest lava flow in recent times poured out of Laki volcano in Iceland, in 1783. It flowed for a distance of 70 kilometres before grinding to a halt.

6 The longest-lasting lava flow came from Kilauea on Hawaii. The volcano erupted non-stop from February 1972 to July 1974, a grand total of 901 days. It spewed out enough lava to fill 100,000 Olympic swimming-pools.

7 Talking of Kilauea, this is the volcano which Pele, the Hawaiian goddess of fire, calls home, sweet home. She lives in a crater on the summit. The fine, glassy strands of lava which are blown out of the volcano when it erupts are known as Pele's hair.

8 When lava oozes out of the ground, it sounds like a steam train, chugging merrily along. It may even go through tunnels. Sometimes the top of a lava flow sets solid while liquid lava still flows inside. When the lava's gone, a tube or tunnel is left. There's a whole maze of them under honeycombed Hawaii.

9 The nastiest fact about lava is that it can chug along for years and years, then suddenly stop ... and then suddenly start again. So you never know quite where you are.

10 If you're off to the beach on a volcanic island, don't be bamboozled by the jet black sand. This forms when hot lava hits the sea and is shattered into billions of tiny specks. You may not have the beach to yourself. The maleo bird from Indonesia uses the black sand as a nest, burying its eggs in the sand. Here, they're kept wonderfully warm and snug until the chicks hatch out.

Violently funny volcanologist's joke

A pillow lava is a type of lava which comes from underwater volcanoes. It billows out of cracks in the seabed, cools very quickly in the cold water and solidifies into rocky blobs.

Watch out if you're thinking of snuggling up to a piece of pillow lava. It's not soft, or comfy.

Awful ash

Lava's not the only horrible hazard from volcanoes. Some violent volcanoes blast out clouds of choking, clogging red-hot ash and dust, tens of kilometres into the air. The ash is made of superfine fragments of lava and rock, like chalk or flour, and there's millions and millions of tonnes of it. Some of it's carried far away. Some settles closer to home. And, that's when problems begin. It buries towns and fields for miles around, making it horribly hard even to breathe.

When Japan's Mt Unzen suddenly erupted in 1991, even the street lights were fooled when a vast cloud of ash blotted out the sun, turning day to night in towns all around. So fooled, they all came on. But if they thought that was bad, they probably hadn't reckoned on the...

Perilous pyroclastic flows

Without doubt, the worst hazards of all from volcanoes are pyroclastic flows. These happen when an ash cloud collapses, and pours and rolls down the mountainside like a glowing, ashy, gassy avalanche, hugging the ground and sweeping rocks and trees away. For anything in the killer flow's path, there is NO ESCAPE. Pyroclastic flows are...

1 FAST! Travelling at up to 200 kilometres an hour!
2 HOT – from 300°C to 800°C, or even hotter!

3 and DEADLY! A pyroclastic flow from the 1902 eruption of Mt Pelée in Martinique demolished the island's capital city and suffocated its 30,000 inhabitants, in a matter of seconds...

It was a series of deadly pyroclastic flows that did for Pompeii in AD 79. But, strangely, they also saved the town for posterity. By covering the town in a thick layer of ash, it was kept in almost perfect condition until archaeologists unearthed it centuries later. Even down to some ancient Roman loaves of bread.

A more grisly discovery was a group of bodies, frozen for ever in time. These were people who choked to death on the ash. Then the hot ash cooled and set hard round their bodies. Inside, the soft flesh rotted away, leaving only their bones ... and a ghostly, body-shaped hollow. In 1860, an Italian archaeologist working at Pompeii had an idea. He removed the bones and filled the hollows with plaster of Paris. When this hardened, it made a plaster cast which could then be dug out of the rock. Giving us a ghastly glimpse of the past.

Historians and archaeologists had a field day finding out what Roman life was really like. Victims of the volcano would no doubt be delighted to know that they didn't die in vain. Here are just a few of the discoveries from Pompeii...

- What the Romans ate and drank – in the remains of taverns, along the streets and in Roman baths they found: eggs, walnuts, figs, (almost) 2,000-year-old bread (a round loaf marked into eight portions was found still in the bread oven in the bakery).

- What the Romans liked to do – they unearthed a theatre, a temple, a gladiators' barracks and an amphitheatre for gladiator shows.

- What the Romans wore – from mosaics and artefacts they could tell that snake bracelets were all the rage with well-dressed ancient Romans.

SNAKE BRACELET

SNAKE BAFFLED

- What pets the Romans kept – one mosaic showed a picture of a guard dog with the words *Cave Canem* (Beware of the Dog) underneath it; they even found a dog preserved in the ash.

HE DIDN'T EVEN FINISH HIS DINNER

FIDIUS

Lethal lahars

Imagine a massive, squelching river of mud, like thick, hot concrete, hurtling at high speed down a volcano's side and you've got a lahar. What's so lethal about lahars is the speed at which they travel, up to 160 kilometres an hour. They're murderous mud-flows, formed when water from melting ice mixes with volcanic ash. They bury towns and fields, clog rivers, and shove bridges and buildings out of their way.

When Mt Pelée erupted in 1902, a rum factory owner, Dr Guérin, witnessed firsthand the havoc a lahar can cause. It was 12.45 p.m. on 5 May. Dr Guérin was just leaving home...

5 MAY

As I left my house, I heard people shouting, "The mountain's falling down!" Then I heard a noise like nothing on Earth—an immense noise, like the devil. A black avalanche, full of huge blocks, was rolling down the mountain. It left the river bed and rolled against my factory like an army of giant rams. I stood rooted to the spot.

I watched my poor wife and son run towards the shore and prayed for their escape.

Then, all at once, the mud arrived. It passed right in front of me and I felt its deadly breath. There was a great crashing sound and everything was crushed, drowned and submerged. Three black waves swept down, one by one, like thunder towards the sea. My wife and son were swept away. A boat was flung high into the air, killing my trusty foreman.

I cannot describe the desolation.

> In the space of a moment, there was nothing to see but a vast black sea of sludge. All I could see of my factory were its chimneys, sticking out of the deadly mire.

And, by lethal lahar standards, this was quite a low-key affair. When Mt Pinatubo in the Philippines erupted in 1991, the largest lahars ever recorded devastated the surrounding landscape. They left a thousand people dead, a million homeless and acres of the country's most fertile rice fields utterly destroyed. Many people were forced to beg for their living. The mud buried several large cities. Even today, the threat isn't over. Vast amounts of ash still cover the mountain and every autumn, when the monsoon rains fall, it turns to mud and starts to flow...

Red-hot rocks

The rocks made when magma or lava cools and hardens (above or below ground) are called igneous, or fire, rocks. There are many different types. But the most famous fire rock, by a long chalk, is ...

PUMICE!

Looking for that ideal gift? Fed up with giving talc and book tokens? Desperately seeking something different? Then look no further. We have the answer to your prayers. Say goodbye for ever to dull old rubber ducks, with an ...

Pumice floats because it's full of hot air. Well, bubbles of gas to be horribly technical. That's why it's full of holes, left when the bubbles go pop. Violent volcanoes blast out millions of tonnes of pimply pumice, from tiny pieces the size of peas to blocks as big as icebergs. Honestly. When Krakatoa erupted in 1883, ships spent months dodging huge hazardous pumice-bergs floating on the sea.

Bright lightning

You often see brilliant flashes of lightning during a violent eruption. This is how they happen.

1 Millions of minuscule fragments of lava and dust whizz round inside an awesome ash cloud...

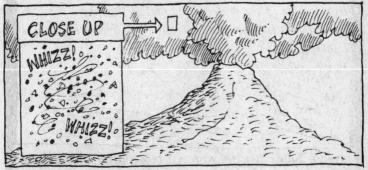

2 ... and rub together frighteningly fast.

3 This makes static electricity (the sort you get if you comb your hair very quickly) ...

4 ... which shoots out of the cloud as bolts of lightning.

BOLT!

BOLT!

BOLT!

BOLTING FOR COVER

Earth-shattering fact

And now for those fish. Believe it or not, when Mt Tungurahua in Ecuador erupted in 1886, a rain of fish fell on the nearby plains. The fish were thought to have come from a lake in the crater. Apparently, they were none the worse for their strange ordeal, not even slightly battered or lightly fried.

Violent volcanic vocab quiz

Is your geography teacher exploding with volcanic knowledge? Try this quiz on them to find out.

1 What is a'a?

a) the noise you'd make running away from a lava flow

b) a sharp type of rock that cuts easily – best not to touch it with your bare hands

c) a Hawaiian word for lava

2 Where would you find a vug?

a) stopping up a small crater

b) in a volcanologist's rucksack

c) inside a volcanic rock

3 What are lapilli?

a) small bits of rock and lava that blast out of volcanoes

b) small bits of gold found in volcanoes

c) offerings made to volcano gods

4 What would you do with a bread-crust bomb?

a) eat it

b) cook it

c) get out of its way

5 What is pahoehoe?

a) a tool you use to dig through volcanic rock

b) lava in Hawaiian

c) the largest volcano in Hawaii

6 What is a caldera?

a) a circular crater on top of a volcano

b) a circular cone on the side of a volcano

c) a huge pan that old women in pointy black hats are supposed to dance round

7 What is basalt?

a) a volcanic gas

b) a black or grey volcanic rock

c) something you put on your chips

8 What is tuff?

a) a material used to make volcanologists' socks

b) a rock made from volcanic ash

c) a type of grass that can grow on lava

9 What is a fumarole?

a) a type of smoked fish

b) an instrument for measuring fumes

c) a steaming hole in the ground

10 What is a maars?

a) the next planet to Earth

b) a type of volcano

c) a glacier on top of a volcano

Answers:

1 c) A'a (ah-ah) is thick, sticky lava which forms jagged, chunky rock when it cools. So sharp it can cut the soles off your boots.

2 c) A vug is a hole in a volcanic rock, often lined with crystals. Most vugs are quite small but a cave-sized vug was once discovered. Its crystals filled 1,400 sacks.

3 a) Ranging from pea-sized to apple-sized. Their name means little stones in Latin. Bet your teacher didn't know that!

4 c) A bread-crust bomb is a round blob of lava chucked out of a volcano. It gets its name because as it flies through the air, the outside cools and hardens while the inside stays hot and gooey. This cracks the hard crust, like a loaf of freshly-baked bread – but don't try to cook or eat it. Running away is definitely the most sensible option.

5 b) Pahoehoe (pa-hoy-hoy) is runny, fast-flowing lava. Looks like smooth, curly coils of rope when it cools.

6 a) Volcanically speaking, a caldera's a very large crater blasted out when a volcano erupts or when a volcano caves in on itself. But if you want to be clever you could give a mark for c), since caldera is also Spanish for cauldron. Calderas often fill with rainwater to make lofty volcanic lakes. Some are tens of kilometres across.

7 b) There are lots of different types of volcanic rocks. Basalt is the most common.

8 b) Very useful for building.

9 c) Found wherever volcanoes are, it spurts steam and smelly gases and is often ringed with crusty yellow sulphur crystals.

10 b) A small volcano formed when magma heats water underground and it explodes to the surface as steam. Absolutely nothing to do with the planet Mars.

What your teacher's score means:

0-4 Oh dear! Sounds like this geography teacher could be nearing "extinction".

5-7 Better. Your teacher's no expert but they obviously know their basalt from their table salt.

8-10 Bravo! Your teacher is obviously "active", and perhaps even a secret volcanologist. Watch out if they start letting off steam.

Of course, apart from being mad, bad and dangerous, volcanoes are fascinating places to visit. So, armed with a smattering of fluent volcano, where on Earth should you start your tour?

Violent Volcano Visitor

Tired of all that homework? Looking for a chance to get away? Despite all the hazards, visiting a violent volcano can be horribly exciting. Horribly dangerous? Possibly. Horribly hard to get to? Probably. But don't let any of that put you off. For the first-time traveller, choosing which violent volcano to visit can be extremely tricky. So, to help you plan your trip of a lifetime, *The Daily Globe* is proud to present the following ghastly guide. Enjoy your horribly hot holiday!

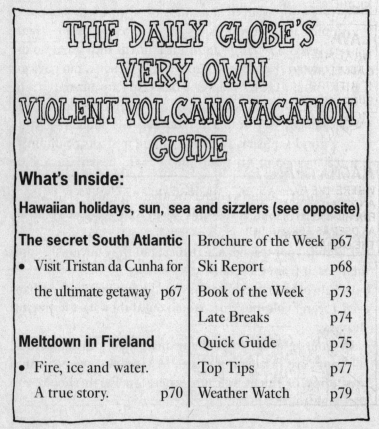

THE DAILY GLOBE'S VERY OWN VIOLENT VOLCANO VACATION GUIDE

What's Inside:

Hawaiian holidays, sun, sea and sizzlers (see opposite)

Happy hot holiday in Hawaii

Beautiful black sandy beaches

With more than five million tourists a year, Hawaii's always a hit with the volcano visitor. But what on Earth makes Hawaii so hot? We sent our roving explorer to find out...

I'd always had a hankering to go to Hawaii and now I seized my chance. I wasn't about to be disappointed. The Hawaiian islands are the tops of gigantic volcanoes formed over a hot spot in the Pacific Ocean. Horribly huge but gentle giants. When they erupt, as they often do, they ooze out lava. Oodles and oodles of the sticky stuff, pouring away in great red-hot rivers or filling the air with fireworks. Awesome.

On my second day in Hawaii, I couldn't wait any longer. It was time to go and see an eruption for myself. I went by bus (you can also go by car or helicopter). The fee includes transport, entry into the Hawaii

Me in front of bus!

National Park, a snack at Volcano House cafe and a guided tour. (If you want a T-shirt, it's extra.) For this, you can see the lava bubbling up from the ground and visit a spot where it sizzles into the sea.

With more than 100 islands to choose from,

Watch those bubbles - phew!

you'll be spoilt for choice in hot spot Hawaii. Don't miss Kilauea which has erupted non-stop since 1983. And do make a detour to Mauna Loa, the largest active volcano in the world. Or if you fancy a spot of night viewing, head for the observatory on (dormant) Mauna Kea.

All too soon, it was time to head home. But I'll be back. For the first-time volcano watcher, Hawaii's a must, a horribly exciting chance to see the Earth in action.

PICK OF THE WEEK

Desperate to get away from it all? Try a trip to tiny Tristan da Cunha, the South Atlantic's hidden gem

★ Wonder at its wide open spaces – only 400 people in the whole place.

★ Bask in blissful peace and quiet – Tristan da Cunha's miles from anywhere. In fact, it's the most isolated island on Earth, about 2,000 km from its nearest neighbours. If you don't believe me, look it up on a map. It's midway between South America and South Africa in the South Atlantic Ocean.

★ Gasp at tales of its last eruption in October 1961. It's actually the tip of an underwater volcano that rises 2,057m above the sea. And just one in a long chain of undersea volcanoes which snakes right up the Atlantic to Iceland, along a crack where two plates of crust pull apart.

★ Enjoy our special offer price – it's excellent value for money. If two of you travel, the third can go free. You'll probably need the company! Call now for a booking form.

THE CASCADE VOLCANOES
YOU KNOW THEY'RE ONLY SLEEPING...

For volcano watching like never before, visit the Cascade Mountains of north-west USA. Snow-capped peaks, fabulous forests, crystal-clear crater lakes and much, much more. See high-rise Mt Rainier and its 26 glaciers. Marvel at mind-blowing Mt St Helens. Feel the earth shake on hair-raising Mt Hood.

SEND FOR YOUR FREE BROCHURE NOW

Come to the Cascades - they're really cookin'

SKI REPORT

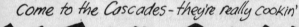

For crisp white snow and stunning scenery, visit Mt Ruapehu (which means "the exploding pit" in Maori) on New Zealand's North Island. The number one ski spot this year. It's the highest mountain on New Zealand, a towering 2,797m tall. Ideal for beginners and experts alike.

HORRIBLE HEALTH WARNING

Expect delays if Mt Ruapehu erupts. Last time it did so, in June 1996, ski slopes, roads and nearby airports were forced to close because of falling ash. Listen out for news bulletins on radio and TV.

COMPETITION

Your chance to win a week's geyser watching in fabulous Yellowstone National Park! A geyser is a giant jet of scalding water and steam that's heated to boiling point by hot volcanic rocks sizzling away underground. You'll find them in places like Iceland and New Zealand, too.

But Yellowstone National Park, Wyoming, USA, is home to the most famous, and most enormous, geyser in the world: Steamboat Geyser. This beauty regularly gushes 115m high. But don't worry if you miss it – there are another 2,999 geysers in the park to watch out for. Another old favourite, Old Faithful, has let off steam every hour for the last 100 years.

Yellowstone Park is sitting on top of a hot spot which is slowly moving under America (it is so slow, it moves at a rate of 3.5cm every year). This is why the rocks underneath it are red hot and that's why those gushing geysers know how to blow.

TO ENTER OUR FABULOUS COMPETITION, FIRST SEE IF YOU CAN ANSWER THESE THREE MIND-BENDING QUESTIONS, THEN COMPLETE THE TIE-BREAK

1: Where is the World's highest geyser?
2: What is it called?
3: Why does a geyser blow?

complete this sentence in no more than 10 words:

"Steamboat is my Kinda geyser because..."

HORRIBLE HOLIDAYS = *taking you close to the edge!*

Meltdown in Fireland

With more than 200 active volcanoes, Iceland's one of the shakiest places on Earth. More Fireland than Iceland, with an eruption every five years – it's a must for every volcano watcher. Iceland's scientists thought they'd seen it all. Until, that is, the dramatic events of autumn 1996, when something sinister seemed to be stirring beneath the ice...

ICELAND
AREA: 103,000 sq. km
POPULATION: 249,000

VATNAJÖKULL

GRIMSVÖTN

REYKJAVIK

For six long weeks, scientists had been monitoring the ghastly Grimsvötn volcano, flying back and forth in an observer plane. The warning signs were already there, with a tell-tale series of earthquakes showing magma stirring deep underground. It seemed the volcano was getting ready to blow. But that wasn't all. Above the volcano lay Vatnajökull, the largest glacier in Europe, covering one-tenth of the island. If the heat of the volcano melted the ice, it could trigger off the most terrible floods Iceland had ever known. The anxious, scientists held their breath, and watched...

ANXIOUS SCIENTISTS

Then, one day, their worst fears were realized. Cracks appeared in the smooth, icy face of the glacier – the earth-shattering eruption had begun. Beneath the ice, the volcano was boiling, melting an incredible 6,000 tonnes of ice every second. By day three of the eruption, its awesome energy had blasted through 760m of ice and melted a vast, yawning chasm in the ice, 3km wide, which belched out black clouds of steam and ash.

The scientists were baffled. They had seen the ice melt with their own eyes but where on Earth had all the water gone? The emergency teams braced themselves for the onslaught, working round the clock to put up barriers to halt the huge flow of water. Parts of the south coast were closed to traffic. Suddenly, almost three weeks later, they got their answer. As if a huge dam had burst, the dreaded flood came. Four billion tonnes of water poured out of the glacier, at a startling speed of 55,000 tonnes a second.

DAM BURST

It tore icebergs the size of houses from the glacier, and swept away roads, bridges, power stations and electricity lines. Eventually, it sped out to sea, leaving fields of icebergs stranded on the shore. The worst was over. When the scientists came to survey the damage, the full force of the massive flood became clear. It was Iceland's worst flood for 60 years, but the Icelanders were lucky! Vatnajökull lies in the empty south of Iceland. The few hundred people who lived near by had already been evacuated. Though millions of pounds of damage were caused, incredibly, no human lives were lost.

ONE LUMP OR TWO? ICELAND'S UNWANTED ICEBERGS

Iceland is one of the most horribly shaky places on Earth. This is because it lies astride two plates of the Earth's crust, one carrying North America and the other, Europe and Asia. Slowly but surely, the plates are moving apart, by 4cm every year. So Iceland, as well as the Earth, is literally being torn apart.

KRAKATOA: THERE SHE BLOWS
by Captain E. Ruption

Based on an eyewitness account, *Krakatoa: There She Blows* tells the story of the most violent volcanic eruption ever. On 27 August 1883, after slumbering quietly for 200 years, Krakatoa, a volcanic island in south-west Indonesia, suddenly exploded. Ash and pumice blasted 50 km into the air. Two-thirds of the island slumped into the sea. The captain of a passing cargo ship watched Krakatoa blow. He noted in his log:

"The deafening explosions sounded like gunfire while lumps of gas-charged lava exploded in the sky, like a gigantic firework display. Just after 5 p.m. the ship's decks were bombarded with hot pumice; some pieces were as large as pumpkins. Ash fell so rapidly on the decks that the crew worked non-stop to keep them clear."

Miraculously, the captain and crew survived. Others weren't so lucky. The explosion triggered a huge tsunami, or tidal wave, which raced towards the low-lying coasts of Java and Sumatra. 163 villages were swept away. A staggering 36,000 people died.

In this gripping book, Captain E. Ruption paints a vivid picture of that dreadful day. Ideal reading for your horrible holiday. (Unless you're off to Indonesia, perhaps. You don't want to push your luck.) Highly recommended.

LATE BREAKS

Cotopaxi

(cot-oh-pak-see), Ecuador
Adventure awaits you in the Andes.
Must be fit – Cotopaxi is 5,897 metres high. If you're feeling lazy, you can go halfway up by car, then cycle down! Honestly! Phase: Active.

Popocatepetl

(pop-oh-cat-a-pet-ul), Mexico
But you can call it Popo, for short. This snow-capped peak is 5,452 metres high and last erupted in 1997. Local legend says Popo was a giant whom the gods turned to stone. Try nearby Mexico City for places to stay. Phase: Dormant.

Etna, Sicily, Italy

Europe's largest active volcano, Mt Etna towers 3,340 metres tall. You can get to the top by bus or car. If you decide to walk, you'll be in good company – one of the first people to climb Mt Etna was the hardy Roman emperor, Hadrian. Last major eruption 1991–1993. Small eruption at the beginning of 1998, so take a hard hat. Phase: Active.

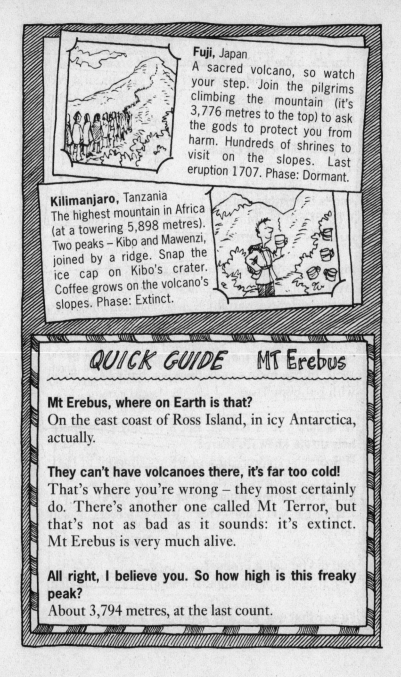

Fuji, Japan
A sacred volcano, so watch your step. Join the pilgrims climbing the mountain (it's 3,776 metres to the top) to ask the gods to protect you from harm. Hundreds of shrines to visit on the slopes. Last eruption 1707. Phase: Dormant.

Kilimanjaro, Tanzania
The highest mountain in Africa (at a towering 5,898 metres). Two peaks – Kibo and Mawenzi, joined by a ridge. Snap the ice cap on Kibo's crater. Coffee grows on the volcano's slopes. Phase: Extinct.

QUICK GUIDE   MT Erebus

Mt Erebus, where on Earth is that?
On the east coast of Ross Island, in icy Antarctica, actually.

They can't have volcanoes there, it's far too cold!
That's where you're wrong – they most certainly do. There's another one called Mt Terror, but that's not as bad as it sounds: it's extinct. Mt Erebus is very much alive.

All right, I believe you. So how high is this freaky peak?
About 3,794 metres, at the last count.

Hmmm, quite a size. And does it still breathe fire?
Very much so. Beneath its icy exterior, it's red hot and raring to go – you can tell by the steam pouring out of its top.

So when did it last erupt?
2006.

And is it horribly violent?
Well, it can be, but it doesn't get many visitors, so no one's usually around to see it.

Phew, so no danger to humans then?
Well, it has had its moments. In 1979, a plane carrying sightseers from New Zealand crashed into Mt Erebus, killing everyone on board.

Sounds violent to me. What's so special about it?
Well, in the main crater there's a big lake ... filled with bubbling lava.

Wow, now you're talking. But if nobody goes there, how do we know it's there?
A Scottish explorer, Sir James Ross, found it in 1841.

Lucky Sir James. What was he doing there?
Exploring, you idiot. That's what explorers usually do.

And did he call it Erebus?
Yes, after one of his ships. It's another word for Hell.

I'd say that was a pretty appropriate name!

AUNTIE VI'S TOP TEN TRAVELLERS' TIPS

It's all very well you going off on these exciting adventures, but you know how much your Auntie Vi worries about you. So, I've put together a few essential tips to make your journey safer. I simply *won't* let you go if you're not prepared!

AUNTIE VI

1 If the volcano you're visiting is active, do BE CAREFUL, luvies – it could quickly turn nasty. Always consult the experts first, will you do that for me? They'll show you a nice safe place to watch from.

2 Now, I know it's hot up those volcanoes, but you must promise to wrap up. You'll need several extra layers of clothes to put on – a nice, thick thermal vest would be ideal, dears. Yes, it might start off warm at the foot of a volcano but, mark my words, it can get ever so nippy at the top.

WRONG!

3 You must watch out for those moving lava flows, and whatever you do, DON'T WALK OVER ONE! Well, they sometimes look rock solid on top, but believe me, underneath, the rocks'll be bubbling more fierily than one of my pepperoni hot pots. You could really put your foot in it.

4 Thick-soled boots are a must, luvie. Yes, even in summer. Volcanic rock can be sharp as razors; it'd slice right through those flimsy trainer things you wear so much.

5 Geysers and hot springs. Now, they're lovely to look at, aren't they, luvies, but always, always, STICK TO THE PATHS. You never know when a thin crust of rock might be hiding a pool of scorching water. Put one foot wrong and you'll be boiled alive. Then you'll be sorry you didn't listen to your Auntie Vi!

6 If you're near a volcano that's even thinking about producing a pyroclastic flow, GET OUT FAST! It will *always* win, luvies.

7 Now if you make it safely to the crater, watch out for volcanic domes that can grow inside. Sometimes they'll just suddenly explode without warning, darlings! Never *ever* go near one that's less than ten years old.

8 It might sound obvious, but I'll mention this one just in case – don't camp near streams running from volcanoes. You wouldn't really want to be swept away by a flood or lava now, would you, luvies?

9 And you'd best avoid craters that are full of gas,

too. Those volcanic gases can be horribly poisonous. You might not be able to hold your breath for long enough to get away. Oh, dear, I can't bear to think of it.

10 Finally, if you must go, always treat volcanoes, violent or otherwise, with respect, luvies. After all, you can never tell what they're up to. Oh, and don't forget to send a postcard to your Auntie Vi, will you? You know how anxious I get.

WEATHER WATCH

When choosing your volcanic vacation, don't forget that volcanoes can seriously damage the weather.

A violent eruption can throw so much ash, dust and gas into the air that it blocks out the sun and lowers temperatures around the world for years afterwards. In 1816, one year after the catastrophic eruption of Tambora in Indonesia, Europe had its coldest summer for almost 200 years. And in North America temperatures fell by 6°C. The wintry weather killed off crops and caused widespread hunger, death and disease, becoming known as 'the year without summer'.

Going on holiday is one thing. But would you want to live on a live volcano? You might be surprised. There are plenty of people who do just that.

Fancy having a volcano for your next-door neighbour? No? Well, millions of people can't be wrong. Or can they? About a tenth of the world's population (500 million people) currently live near an active volcano. Why do they do it? Is it worth the risk? What happens if the volcano turns nasty? Let's have a look at the pros and cons.

Killer mountains?

First, the cons. However you look at it, having your home next to a volcano can be horribly hazardous...

- In the 20th century alone, about 70,000 people have been killed in eruptions.
- Lethal lava can burn and bulldoze everything in its path.
- Choking ash and mud can smother the countryside, devastating farmers' fields and crops, cutting off communications and bringing transport to a halt. In a violent eruption, you stand to lose your home, your livelihood ... and your life. Overnight, a volcano can turn your world into a wasteland. It can take a region hundreds of years to recover. If it ever does.
- There can be sinister side-effects on the world's weather, too, like tsunamis (remember Krakatoa?), starvation and disease. And it can cost millions and millions of pounds to clean up the mess.

And then there's the awful uncertainty. Violent volcanoes are horribly unpredictable. One minute, you're happily living in paradise. The next, your world's been turned upside-down. As the people of Montserrat, a tiny, beautiful tropical island in the sunny Caribbean, found to their cost in July 1995, when Chance's Peak, a dormant volcano in the south of the island, suddenly woke up ...

TROUBLE IN PARADISE

ROSE'S DIARY

18 JULY 1995

KEEP OUT!

Dear Diary

Strange things are happening in my town. On our way back from school today, we were playing I-spy. My sister spotted something beginning BS. After what seemed like ages, I gave up, and she said "Black snow', you idiot!" She is only eight and she's got a wild imagination! So I played along with her, but then I saw what she meant. It looked like smoke was coming from the Soufriere Hills behind the town - they're more like mountains really - and big specks of ash were starting to fall from the sky. It really did look like black snow. It doesn't usually snow at all on Montserrat, so I started to feel really spooked.

My sister

After tea we raced over to grandma's. She knows everything there is to know, so we asked her why the mountain was smoking.

"Oh, you don't need to worry about that, girls," she said "The scientists will sort it out. That's what they're paid for. That old volcano's been fast asleep for 400 years and it's not about to wake up now."

Grandma

Still I couldn't remember seeing anything like the smoke and the snow before, and I have been around for a whole ten years.

20 July 1995

We haven't been to school for two days now. So it has to be serious. The volcano is starting to erupt. First it started to rumble, then huge rocks and stones started shooting out of the top. Like this.
Even in the middle of the day, it got really dark. Mr Dyer, our next door neighbour, was dead nervous - I've never seen him like that before.

He's got some fields on the mountain side where he grows sweet potatoes and carrots and keeps his goats. He can't go and visit them now, though, it's far too risky. I wonder what the goats must be thinking? My Mum tried her best to calm him down but she didn't sound convincing - her voice went all wobbly and that's usually bad news.

where's my dinner?

Mr Dyer looking worried

Mum, going all wobbly

26 July 1995

Things are getting worse and worse. Our house is now covered in thick, black ash - and half the town is too. It's horrible. I daren't breathe too deeply in case I swallow some of it. When we turned on the T.V., a man was saying that the volcano could erupt at any time now...
What's going to happen to us all?

26 August 1995

The volcano was still huffing and blowing and things got really bad. In the end, the government said it was too dangerous for people to carry on living in Plymouth - that's the capital of Montserrat, and where I live!

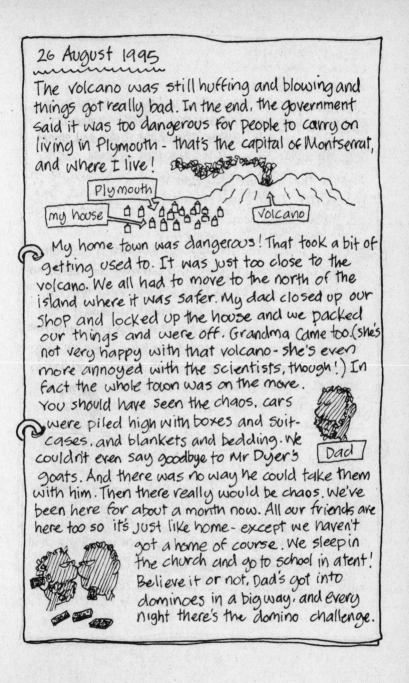

Plymouth

my house

Volcano

My home town was dangerous! That took a bit of getting used to. It was just too close to the volcano. We all had to move to the north of the island where it was safer. My dad closed up our shop and locked up the house and we packed our things and were off. Grandma came too.(she's not very happy with that volcano- she's even more annoyed with the scientists, though!) In fact the whole town was on the move. You should have seen the chaos, cars were piled high with boxes and suit-cases, and blankets and bedding. We couldn't even say goodbye to Mr Dyer's

Dad

goats. And there was no way he could take them with him. Then there really would be chaos. We've been here for about a month now. All our friends are here too so it's just like home- except we haven't got a home of course. We sleep in the church and go to school in a tent! Believe it or not, Dad's got into dominoes in a big way, and every night there's the domino challenge.

14 March 1997

We're still in the camp. It's like a little town now with its own shop which Dad runs and a hospital. We moved out of the church into a wooden house. It's quite nice but a bit squashed. Everyone's squashed here, though. Some people who live in huge houses have to share their luxury bedrooms. Some people even got to stay in tourist hotels and holiday homes - my Dad says they still have to pay, even though it isn't much of a holiday.

Last night there was a gospel concert in one of the hotels. It was great, just like church used to be on Sundays: I really thought the roof might lift off! They made such a beautiful sound. It's funny how people can be so cheerful when everything seems to be going wrong. Grandma says people are just, "putting a brave face on things" and deep down we're all a bit fed up. My Mum says, "you have to laugh, or else you cry."

The volcano is STILL erupting. Poor Mr Dyer's fields have all gone. They've been buried in ash and rock. Now he doesn't know what he'll do. (I'm trying not to think about the goats.) And lots of people have got bad coughs from breathing in all the ash. I've stopped asking when we can go home - I think it was getting on mum's nerves. And we might not be able to - ever! It all depends on the volcano. And no one knows what it'll do!

me and my sister

21 March 1997

I had a dream last night that everything was O.K. We were living back home and everything was normal. The mango tree in the garden was bursting with fresh, juicy fruit. I was at my old school and all my old friends were there as if nothing had happened. The sky was a deep blue, the hill sides were rich green and dotted with orange and yellow flowers, just like they used to be. I felt great when I woke up, but then I remembered where I was, and what one man said yesterday - "Everything back home is grey. It looks like you've walked into a black and white photograph." - and I knew we would never go back.

21 July 1997 - London, England

Such a lot has happened in the last few months that I haven't had time to write. One day, my Dad came home from the shop and told us he'd made a decision. We were leaving Montserrat and going to England to live. Lots of people had already gone and others had gone to Antigua. Next thing I knew we were on a boat sent from England and off on our journey across the world. Me and my sister cried and cried as the boat pulled out of the harbour.

85

Montserrat looked beautiful as we left, but when we got further away, we could see smoke and I knew we had to go. Grandma decided to stay behind. She said she was much too old to start travelling now. And anyway, the volcano might go quiet again. It hasn't yet! It's still erupting and there could be a really big explosion any day now.

It's OK living with my Uncle in London and going to a new school but all I want is to go home. It's so cold here! And I miss so many things. These are just a few of them:

❀ The steaming heat that cools down when the rain comes.

❀ Squidging black sand through my toes on the beaches (we used to walk to the beach from our house). It's because of the volcano that the sand's black.

❀. The tropical turquoise sea and catching fish with my dad.

❀ Friday night street parties (I used to watch them from my bedroom window).

❀ Dressing up for church on Sunday.

Goatwater stew and Grandma's sugar cake - made from fresh coconut, yum.

But most of all, I miss my Grandma.

goatwater stew

sugar cake

> I suppose I'll get used to living here, but I can't help my dreams about being at home, and I can't help feeling disappointed when I wake up.
>
> Rosie   age 12½

Big, friendly giants?

Given the danger, why on Earth would anyone choose to live near an active volcano? You might be surprised.

Magma, Lava & Ash, Estate Agents

FOR SALE

One house, slightly ashy. Great views over the valley. Steeply sloping, terraced garden. With built-in volcano-proof bunker. Some subsidence likely.

Some red-hot reasons for living near a volcano

1 Fabulously fertile soil. Volcanic soil is the richest on Earth. Especially after a light dusting of ash. And chock-full of nourishment to help plants prosper. From ancient times, volcanoes have been heavily farmed and today provide food for millions of people.

TERRACE FARMING

FARMER

ASH

TERRACE

Some of the best rice-growing land in Indonesia, for example, lies in the shadow of active volcanoes. It's so fantastically fertile, farmers can grow three crops, not one, every year. Since the days of Pompeii, fine wines have come from volcanic vineyards on the slopes of Mt Vesuvius. Not to mention coffee from the craters of Central America. Of course, you can have too much of a good thing. If the ash is too thick, about 20 centimetres or more, it kills fields dead.

2 Cheap central heating. In volcanic regions, underground water gets superheated to 150°C. This can be pumped directly into people's homes for washing and central heating. Or it can be converted into cheap electricity. It's called geothermal energy and it's cheap, clean and won't run out. No wonder geographers love it! It means that in places like icy Iceland, you can take a midwinter dip in a heated swimming-pool. Outdoors! Or eat tropical fruit like bananas and pineapples which are grown in geothermal greenhouses.

3 Loads of lava. Lava is horribly useful. How? For a start, you can...

- live in it. Since the 4th century AD, people in Cappadocia, Turkey, have hollowed out cave-like homes, and even churches, inside lava cones. It's easy to dig, strong, fireproof and an excellent insulator (keeps you warm in winter and cool in summer) to boot. What more could you possibly ask for?

- stone-wash your jeans with it. You know those faded jeans your dad still wears that used to be trendy? Well, the stone they're washed with is ... pumice!
- house-train your cat in it. Lots of cat litter is actually volcanic ash. Great for soaking up those things cats do.
- improve your looks with it. (Well, the looks of your feet anyway.) If hard skin's a problem, get straight to work with a pumice stone. They've been used for centuries. In fact, baffled archaeologists at work on a dig thought the place had been pummelled by pumice during a volcanic eruption. Except that there wasn't a volcano near by. Then, they realized that people had probably been pummelling themselves with pumice stones for centuries to smooth their skin – they'd bought the stones from Roman traders who were a very long way from home.

PUMICE
SLIPPERS
↓

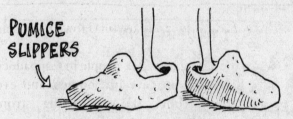

LOSE THAT HARD SKIN AS YOU WALK

4 Brilliant building blocks. Rock made from volcanic ash is tuff by name and tough by nature. Cut into blocks, it's brilliant for building. Houses, roads, bridges, you name it. And concrete. It was the Romans who invented concrete and completely changed building techniques, by building structures that actually stayed standing. And the secret ingredient in concrete? Volcanic dust, as if you hadn't guessed! Without volcanoes, you wouldn't have had such staggering structures as the Colosseum, or the Pantheon or Roman roads that your history teacher is always going on about.

5 Marvellous metals. What do copper, lead, tin, silver and gold have in common? The answer is they're all found in magma. Mining these metals is big business. Though it's best to wait for the volcano to cool. You can also find gold in volcanic hot springs.

6 Gorgeous gemstones. Gemstones don't get more gorgeous than dazzling diamonds. You'll find these sparklers in volcanic rock (called kimberlite). If you're lucky. And if the volcano's been extinct for at least a couple of million years. Diamonds are formed deep inside the Earth and churned up by volcanoes, especially in South Africa and Western Australia. Even more precious is rare red beryl from Utah in the USA. Chip out one little beryl and you could be seriously rich!

RED BERYL FROM UTAH

AUNTIE BERYL FROM BOGNOR

7. Super sulphur. When the sulphur in volcanic gases cools down, it forms crusty crystals that are a brilliant yellow colour. You see them around hot springs and fumaroles. Sulphur is mined in Italy, Chile and Japan. It's used to make matches, gunpowder, dyes and ointments (and it stinks! It's the same stuff that's used to make stink bombs). It's also added to rubber to make it tougher for tyres. This process is called vulcanization, after good old Vulcan.

Earth-shattering fact
If all else fails, why not save on electricity and use your volcano as an oven? That's what villagers on Mt Unzen, Japan do. Forget about egg-timers and boiling water! They use the hot steam gushing out of the volcano to hard-boil eggs for lunch.

Horrible Health Warning

If you're thinking of risking life on the lava, it pays to be careful. Very careful. So, how can you tell if a violent volcano is about to erupt? Here are some warning signs to listen and look out for.

PUFFS OF STEAM AND ASH: WEAK AT FIRST, BUT GETTING STRONGER.

SWELLING: AS MAGMA WELLS, THE VOLCANO SWELLS. WATCH OUT FOR BUMPS AND BULGES APPEARING LIKE MT ST HELENS. (SEE PAGE 9)

SIDE VENTS: ANYTHING TO GET IN ON THE ACTION. OPEN UP AND SPIT OUT LAVA.

HOT SPRINGS AND FUMAROLES: MORE COMMON AS THE HEAT BUILDS UP

FALLING ROCKS: AS THE ROCK FACE CRACKS UNDER THE HEAT AND PRESSURE. ALSO FLOODS AS GLACIERS START TO CRACK UP.

RUMBLING: FROM MASSES OF MINI-EARTHQUAKES. COMMOM BEFORE A VIOLENT ERUPTION. SHOW THAT UNDERGROUND MAGMA IS STARTING TO STIR. (THE HORRIBLY TECHNICAL TERM FOR A MASS OF EARTHQUAKES IS A SWARM. LIKE BEES. SORT OF).

LOUD NOISES: LIKE GUNSHOTS BUT REALLY SMALL EXPLOSIONS. VOLCANOES ALSO ROAR, SPLUTTER, HISS, WHISTLE, GO POP. YOU GET THE PICTURE... ALL THAT COULD REALLY GET ON YOUR NERVES.

Other telltale signs include…
- Barking: it's said that dogs get restless before an eruption!

- Smelly fumes: levels of toxic gases rise with the magma. Very dangerous. By the time these gases get up your nose, it could be too late. Some are smellier than others, e.g. stinky sulphur dioxide which smells like rotten eggs. Some are acids which can bleach or eat your clothes (and skin). But the deadliest of all, carbon dioxide, has no odour. Which makes it horribly hard to detect.

The terrible (true) tale of the killer lake

Night had fallen on 21 August 1986. In the village of Lower Nyos, Cameroon, most people were already fast asleep and did not hear the sound of a small explosion at nearby Lake Nyos. Those who heard it thought nothing of it. Little did they realize the terrible danger they were in.

The noise signalled the release from the lake of a huge cloud of poisonous gases, 50 metres thick. The deadly fumes poured silently down the valley, suffocating 1,700 people. In Lower Nyos alone, 1,200 people died. The handful of survivors told how they had seen people simply drop down dead in the middle of eating or talking. The morning brought another grisly scene – the fields around Lower Nyos were strewn with the bodies of thousands of cattle. For 21 August had been market day. Unusually, no flies or vultures hovered around the bodies. They too had been caught in the killer cloud's path.

The gases came from Lake Nyos, a small, deep lake which had formed inside a volcanic crater. Over hundreds of years, toxic gases leaking from the volcano had collected in the water at the bottom of the lake. The main gas was deadly poisonous carbon dioxide, undetectable because it has no smell. On that fateful August night, something happened in the lake to trigger the release of the gases. Heavy rains or a small earthquake may have stirred up the water, bringing the gases to the surface. But no one knows for certain. Whatever the reasons for the killer cloud, the results were catastrophic. It suffocated every living thing in its path until it was scattered by the wind and rain. Thousands of people fled their homes, too terrified to live by the lake a moment longer.

Sadly, warning signs aren't always reliable. No two volcanoes behave the same. A violent eruption may be minutes, months, or even years away. And there are often false alarms – you never can be certain. Sometimes you get no warning at all, even if you do know what to watch out for...

If a violent volcano blows its top, there's not a lot you can do. Except get out of its way. Fast! If you pick a fight with a volcano, the volcano will always win. Well, almost always. A few brave souls have taken on volcanoes and won. Others have tried ... but failed. Others are still trying. Very trying.

The Daily Globe
12 May 1902, Martinique, West Indies
PRISONER IN ERUPTION ESCAPE SHOCK

In the aftermath of last week's devastating eruption, a shocked prisoner is today celebrating a miraculous escape from death. In an interview with this paper, the man, Auguste Ciparis, told our reporter, "I must be the luckiest man alive."

PRISONER SET FREE

Very lucky indeed. Condemned to die at dawn on 9 May, Ciparis was spending his final days in a dungeon-like cell under St Pierre jail. Lucky because, in the once-bustling town of St Pierre, he was one of only two people left alive.

Meanwhile, the island is struggling to come to terms with the terrible tragedy. Mt Pelée, dormant for centuries, had shown signs of stirring for several weeks. In mid-April, a sugar refinery high on the slopes was destroyed in a minor eruption. On 25 April a shower of ash fell like ghostly snow on St Pierre, turning day to night. But the authorities still said there was nothing to fear. Then, at 7.45 a.m., on 8 May, the sleeping volcano began to wake up. The whole shattering event was witnessed by Fernand Clerc, a wealthy farmer from St Pierre. On a hunch, he and his family had packed up and left town. They were the only ones to do so. From a safe distance, they watched in horror as the whole south side of the mountain suddenly blew apart, blasting out a huge

MT PELEE BLOWS ITS TOP

rolling black cloud.

"It was like a thousand enormous cannon," Mr Clerc told us. "Firing out scorching steam and rocks."

He went on to describe to me how, before their terrified eyes, this hellish cloud of ash, rock and fire (known technically as a pyroclastic flow) hurtled down the mountainside at incredible speed, "like a red-hot hurricane of fire". It swallowed up everything in its path.

In seconds, it reached St Pierre. There was no way of escape. Some people were suffocated. Others were buried. Others were burned to death. All but two of the town's 30,000 inhabitants perished (apart from Ciparis, another man survived simply by hiding beneath his workbench). Then the deadly cloud flowed into the sea where it made the water hiss and boil. In the harbour, ships were torn from their moorings and flung out to sea.

For seven terrible hours the nightmare continued.

ST PIERRE IN RUINS

Among the burned-out ruins of St Pierre, Auguste Ciparis was found four days later, in his cell, still calling weakly for help. Perhaps the only one for whom the volcano brought good fortune, he has since been granted his freedom – both his accusers and would-be executioners are now dead.

Then Mt Pelée at last grew quiet once more.

Earth-shattering fact
Fer de lance snakes are some of the most vicious vipers in the world. They usually live in the rainforests of South and Central America. The fer de lance will only sink its enormous fangs into human flesh if it's disturbed – but when it does bite, the victim dies. (It's incredible, then, that some local people used to catch the snakes and fire them at their enemies, using a special blow-pipe.) When Mt Pelée erupted, 50 people were killed by deadly fer de lance snakes which had been disturbed by all the mess and din.

Saved by the cell
The violent eruption of Mt Pelée ranks as one of the 20th century's worst volcanic disasters. As for Auguste Ciparis? He later became a bit of a celebrity, touring the world as a circus act. (He called himself Ludger Sylbaris. For some

reason!) He owed his life to the thick stone walls of his cell. Many years later, this gave scientists a good idea... Using Ciparis's cell as a model, they designed a new type of volcano shelter. To make your own, here's what to do.

What you need:
- a large concrete pipe about 2 metres wide
- a hillside (volcanic)

What you do:
1 Bury the pipe in the hillside like this:

2 Add a door at the end.

3 Stock up on tinned food, bedding, books, gas masks, tin opener etc.

4 At the first sign of an eruption, take cover. Simple!

But even when you think you're in the perfect position to avoid a volcano, you may not be as safe as you think. You might think that a jet plane would be the perfect place to be, but you'd be wrong...

98

Almost a mid-air dis-ash-ter

"Good evening, ladies and gentlemen, this is your captain, Eric Moody, speaking. We hope you enjoyed your evening meal. You might be interested to know that, although it's dark outside, if you look through your window, the lights you can see below are on the island of Sumatra, Indonesia. We're now heading towards Java, cruising at a height of 11,500 metres. We're set for a comfortable few hours' journey, so sit back and enjoy the in-flight movie."

Everything seemed perfectly normal.

It was 24 June, 1982. British Airways Flight 9, a Boeing 747-200, was en route from Malaysia to Perth, Australia, with 247 passengers and 16 crew on board. And they were all in for a terrible shock.

Captain Moody had just left his seat to talk to the passengers, when his co-pilot called him back to the flight deck. Through the cockpit window, they could see a dazzling display of lightning, like an incredible fireworks display. A breathtaking sight, they agreed.

Then came a series of extraordinary events. First, the number four engine failed – this wasn't especially unusual, and as there were another three engines, the crew weren't especially worried. But then, inexplicably, one after the other, the other three engines failed. In the space of a minute, all four engines had stopped running. The impossible had happened.

Quickly, the captain sent out a mayday call.

"Jakarta, Jakarta. Mayday! Mayday! This is Speedbird 9. We have lost all engines. Repeat, we have lost all engines!"

The first the passengers knew of the danger that faced them was when the beam from the movie projector seemed to fill up with smoke with no sign of a fire. Captain Moody made a short announcement: "Ladies and gentlemen, we have a small problem. We've lost all four engines. We're doing our damnedest to get them going again. We hope you're not in too much distress."

Gradually, the smoke got thicker until the oxygen masks came down. Then all the lights went out in the cabin. Over the next few minutes, the plane plunged thousands of metres through the air as the crew tried in vain to restart the engines.

The terrified passengers sat in pitch darkness, and in silence, except for the eerie creaking of the fuselage. For, with no power, there was no air conditioning, and no noise. They felt sure they were going to die.

For 16 heart-stopping minutes, the plane fell. It seemed an eternity, but then, at about 4,000 metres, one of the engines suddenly restarted. Closely followed by another. And, at the last minute, the third and fourth engines started with a mighty roar. It wasn't only the engines that roared. Their was a roar from the passengers too; some had tears streaming down their faces. Their relief was overwhelming.

The crew prepared for an emergency landing at Jakarta airport. Despite poor visibility – the windscreen had been badly sandblasted – the plane landed smoothly, and safely. Thanks to the expertise of the pilots, the badly shocked passengers had a lucky escape.

What Captain Moody didn't know was that the cause of the shut-down was a huge ash cloud, from the eruption of the Galunggung volcano on Java. The plane had flown right through it, sucking choking ash into its engines and causing them to stall.

As the plane fell, the engines restarted because rushing air blew the ash away. But why hadn't the crew spotted the cloud? For a start, it was night, so they couldn't see it, and it didn't show up on the radar screen. And, although Galunggung had been belching out ash for several months now, no one had thought to warn them...

There's no need to panic! Things have got better since then. Pilots are now trained to spot the warning signs. These include St Elmo's fire – the fireworks display the crew spotted, it's a type of lightning formed in an ash cloud when particles of ash rub together and become highly charged with electricity – and a strong stench of sulphur that's just like rotten eggs. Then, instead of **1** speeding up (to try to shake the ash out of the engines) and **2** trying to fly up and out of the cloud (not always possible as some ash clouds rise higher than an airliner can go), they are told to **1** slow down (to lower the temperature inside the engines so the glassy ash doesn't melt and clog them up more) and **2** turn around and fly back out of the cloud.

Meanwhile, back on the ground...

Stopping the flow

Picture the scene... The lava's flowing straight towards you, your home is under threat, all your CDs, and your priceless stamp collection, are about to go up in smoke. You've got to act fast. But what can you do? Is it ever possible to stop the flow? Or even divert it out of harm's way? Here are a few tried and tested methods, but do they work? Decide which method you think works best, then check out the answers on pages 105-7.

1 Build a dam across it. There have been many attempts at diverting lava flows by blocking their path with a wall or barrier. The idea is the lava piles up higher and higher on one side of the wall, then dribbles gently over the top.

2 Take a shovel to it. On Mt Etna, in 1669, workers attacked a lava flow with picks and shovels to try to push it away from their town.

3 Bomb it. Sometimes the top of lava goes cool and crusty while it's still hotly flowing below. So pick your moment, then drop the bomb. The idea is that the bomb breaks the crust and slows down the flow by clogging it up with solid lava chunks. Which makes the lava spill out sideways and weakens the force of the flow. You hope!

4 Hose it down. Use a cold water hose and spray it in the direction of the lava to make it set rock hard. That should stop it in its tracks or at least make it change its course.

In January 1973, the islanders of Heimaey in Iceland watched in horror as a huge crack, 2 kilometres long, opened up on the edge of the main town of Vestmannaeyjar. Within days, the boiling Earth below had built a volcano more than 200 metres high where a tranquil meadow had once been. Thick black ash rained down on the town. Wherever you looked, fires raged. But more omnious still was the huge river of lava creeping slowly but surely towards the harbour. Without the harbour, there would be no fishing industry ... and no Heimaey. Most of the islanders left for safety but one group of men stayed behind, determined to fight back. What on Earth could they do to lure the lava away? The days passed by. Then the weeks. Time was fast running out. Then someone had an idea. They organized a system of fire engines and set to work hosing the lava down with millions of litres of sea water. But would it work?

5 Divert it. When Etna erupted, between 1991 and 1993, valiant volcanologists built a new channel next to the lava flow. Then they used explosives to block the path of the lava. The idea was that the explosives would divert the lava into their home-made channel.

6 Offer it a sacrifice. If all else fails, you could always try a short prayer or a sacrifice. That's what people in Hawaii have done for years. They believe that Kilauea is the home of the fiery goddess, Pele, who lives inside the volcano's crater. You can see her breath in the steam. When she's angry, she stamps her feet and makes the volcano erupt. (She's clearly got a terrible temper – Kilauea erupts almost non-stop.) She also sends out boiling rivers of lava to destroy her enemies. To keep Pele happy (and quiet), people throw offerings into the crater. Could any of these offerings possibly do the trick?

So what does work?
1 Not horribly reliable, but not a bad start. Sometimes it works, but it might burst right through the dam, as

happened when Mt Etna erupted in 1983. But four huge barriers (made of volcanic rock and ash) were strong enough to divert the lava away from many important buildings.

2 Not a good idea if you want to keep on friendly terms with the neighbours, the 1669 operation might have saved one town, but it put another town at risk in the process. There was so much quarrelling, a royal decree had to be passed ordering everyone to leave the lava alone, or else!

3 It's a clever idea. This approach has been used several times in Hawaii. In 1935, a lava tube in a flow from Mauna Loa was bombed. The tube was blown apart and became clogged up with chunks of lava, but scientists couldn't tell if the bombing was effective because the eruption went and stopped anyway. In 1942, the same idea was used at Mount Pele, but local people got upset, as they thought a bomb would offend Pele, the fire goddess and the only person, as far as they were concerned, who could possibly stop the lava flow. (See page 50 for more details about Pele.)

4 Well, it took weeks ... and weeks ... and weeks. But, in the end, to their immense relief (and great astonishment), their perilous plan worked! At Easter, the lava turned. The front of the flow had cooled fast and hardened, forcing the lava behind it to change direction. Not only was the harbour saved, it was better than ever before. The lava lengthened the harbour wall, giving better protection against the waves. The town was rebuilt and the islanders were able to go back home. A happy ending? Until the next time...

5 OK, so it didn't actually stop the flow, but diverting the lava did save the village of Zafferng which is where the lava was originally heading.

6 They have all been used – but did they work? Well, the brandy was especially effective. When Mauna Loa (another

volcano in Pele's charge) erupted in 1881, a lava flow threatened a nearby city. The king's granddaughter was asked to step in. Bold as brass, she stomped straight up to the lava and sprinkled it with a bottle of brandy. And the very next day, it stopped. As for pigs, they're a bit of a love-hate thing. Legend says that Pele almost married Kamapua'a, the pig-man, but it all ended in tears. She told him he was ugly. He put out her fires with fog and rain. The quarrel went on and on. In the end, the gods had to step in and put a stop to it before the whole island was plunged into darkness.

Score one point for each right answer to questions 1–5, and one point for each correct answer in question 6.

Earth-shattering fact
Forget bombs, dams, and bottles of brandy. If you really want to save the day, there's one person who might be able to help ... that's Saint Januarius. He was a bishop in the 3rd century AD who riled the Romans and was thrown to the wild beasts for lunch. But he was so holy that none of the beasts would touch him. Poor old St J was beheaded instead. He later became patron saint of Naples where his skull is kept in a chapel. Except, that is, when Mt Vesuvius looks like erupting. Then it's brought out of hiding and waved in front of the mischievous mountain. Faced with this holy bone, it's said, the volcano goes quiet. At least, it did in 685, 1631 and 1707...

How did you do? Less than four? Well, you know as much as most scientists about volcanoes. Over four, you never know, you might make a brilliant volcanologist. Volcanology isn't all white coats and test-tubes, it's real-life, mind-blowing science...

VIOLENT VOLCANO STUDY

Scientists who study volcanoes are called volcanologists (and yes, they've heard all the jokes about Mr Spock!). All over the world, they're busily trying to get to grips with what makes volcanoes so violent. It's not as easy as it sounds. Studying volcanoes is horribly dangerous. Trickier still is predicting when they might erupt. So why do they do it? Good question. The more we know about volcanoes, the better for everyone. Especially for anyone living near by. Being able to predict eruptions more accurately could save thousands of lives. But the real answer is that, love them or hate them, violent volcanoes are impossible to ignore.

Could you be a vile volcanologist?

Do you have what it takes to become a vile volcanologist? Try this quick quiz to find out.

1 Do you have a head for heights? Yes/No
2 Are you fabulously fit and strong? Yes/No
3 A hot photographer? Yes/No
4 Do you look good in a gas mask? Yes/No

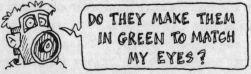

DO THEY MAKE THEM IN GREEN TO MATCH MY EYES?

5 Can you tell the date from a tree ring? Yes/No

ER... IS IT 24 JUNE?

6 Do you know your rocks? Yes/No

7 Are you fond of travelling? Yes/No
8 Are you good at spelling? Yes/No
9 Are you willing to work odd hours? Yes/No
10 Are you mad? Yes/No

How did you do?
8–10 yeses: Excellent! The job's yours if you want it. Read on to find out what to wear.

5–7 yeses: Not bad. But perhaps you'd be better doing something less explosive.

4 yeses and below: Forget it! Volcanology is not for you. Try something else altogether. Like teaching!

Answers:
1 You'll need one – some volcanoes are horribly high. It's a very long way up the world's highest active volcano – Guallatiri in Chile's 6,060 metres high. Its last major eruption was in 1987.

2 You'll need to be – there's a lot of hard climbing involved (see above). If you're woefully weak and feeble, you'll never be able to carry all your horribly heavy equipment. Or the even heavier heaps of rock. Time to build those muscles up!

3 Not essential but useful for showing off afterwards.

4 Like it or not, you'll have to wear one. Volcanoes give off lots of gas, most of it horribly poisonous. And collecting gas samples is a major part of your job.

5 Handy if you can. One of a volcanologist's jobs is finding out about past eruptions. Which might give you a clue to a volcano's future. One way of doing this is to look inside a tree. Each year the trunk grows a new ring. It's usually neat and round. But if the tree's been stunted by falling ash, the ring can be horribly thin and wonky.

6 If you can't tell your basalt from your bath salts, you'll be no good to anyone. As every good volcanologist knows basalt is an igneous (fire) rock made when lava cools. And bath salts are things you put in the bath to make you smell better (some hope).

7 It helps. In your quest to get to know a volcano you could be sent anywhere – from icy Antarctica to hot-spot Hawaii.

8 Again, it helps. Some volcanic vocabulary is horribly hard to spell. Take a phreatomagmatic eruption, for example. (Take it very slowly!) To you and me, that's an eruption of gases and steam, with some mega magma thrown in for good measure.

9 No one knows exactly when or where the next volcano is likely to blow. So a good volcanologist has to be ready to leave home at the drop of a (hard) hat.

10 Not compulsory. But it helps. After all, why else would you do a job where you risked being blown up, burned to a crisp, or thrown at the mercy of a feisty fire god?

110

Dressing the part

If you're going to be a vile volcanologist, you need to dress the part. Safety's more important than looks. Vic is modelling the latest styles in vogue for volcanologists?

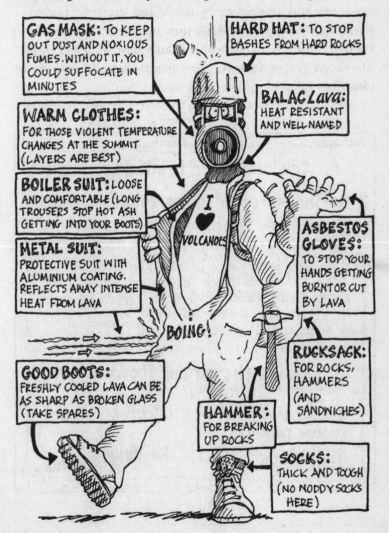

GAS MASK: TO KEEP OUT DUST AND NOXIOUS FUMES. WITHOUT IT, YOU COULD SUFFOCATE IN MINUTES

HARD HAT: TO STOP BASHES FROM HARD ROCKS

BALAC *Lava*: HEAT RESISTANT AND WELL NAMED

WARM CLOTHES: FOR THOSE VIOLENT TEMPERATURE CHANGES AT THE SUMMIT (LAYERS ARE BEST)

BOILER SUIT: LOOSE AND COMFORTABLE (LONG TROUSERS STOP HOT ASH GETTING INTO YOUR BOOTS)

ASBESTOS GLOVES: TO STOP YOUR HANDS GETTING BURNT OR CUT BY LAVA

METAL SUIT: PROTECTIVE SUIT WITH ALUMINIUM COATING. REFLECTS AWAY INTENSE HEAT FROM LAVA

I ♥ VOLCANOES

BOING!

GOOD BOOTS: FRESHLY COOLED LAVA CAN BE AS SHARP AS BROKEN GLASS (TAKE SPARES)

RUCKSACK: FOR ROCKS, HAMMERS (AND SANDWICHES)

HAMMER: FOR BREAKING UP ROCKS

SOCKS: THICK AND TOUGH (NO NODDY SOCKS HERE)

What on Earth does a volcanologist do?
Once Vic has the kit on, he's ready for a piece of the action. He's got one special volcano that he works on. He's come to know it pretty well over the years, by measuring, monitoring, prodding and poking every crack and crevice. There's a whole team of 'Vics' working together on the same volcano and they're all based in an observatory near by. They're a bit like detectives, or doctors, even, except they all work on just one huge patient.

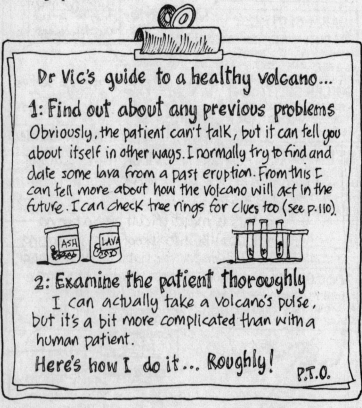

Dr Vic's guide to a healthy volcano...

1: Find out about any previous problems
Obviously, the patient can't talk, but it can tell you about itself in other ways. I normally try to find and date some lava from a past eruption. From this I can tell more about how the volcano will act in the future. I can check tree rings for clues too (see p.110).

2: Examine the patient thoroughly
I can actually take a volcano's pulse, but it's a bit more complicated than with a human patient.
Here's how I do it... Roughly!

P.T.O.

a) Take a couple of gas samples - a volcano gives off more gas just before it erupts.

b) Take its temperature. Mind fingers though - lava can be 1,000°C!

c) Feel for bumps or swellings - signs of magma rising up.

BUMP

d) Listen for any rumblings - these signal earthquakes.

RUMBLE

e) Take some samples of lava and rock.
  I can tell a lot from its age, type and texture.

3: Make your diagnosis
Using all this information I can work out the volcano's 'normal' behaviour. Then I can spot when it starts to act strangely.

4: Find a cure
Ah, yes, this is the difficult bit. So far, no one's come up with a foolproof plan for curing volcanoes of their terrible habit of overflowing. However good your diagnosis, it won't stop the volcano erupting. But you can warn people living nearby to get out of the way... Fast!

RUN!

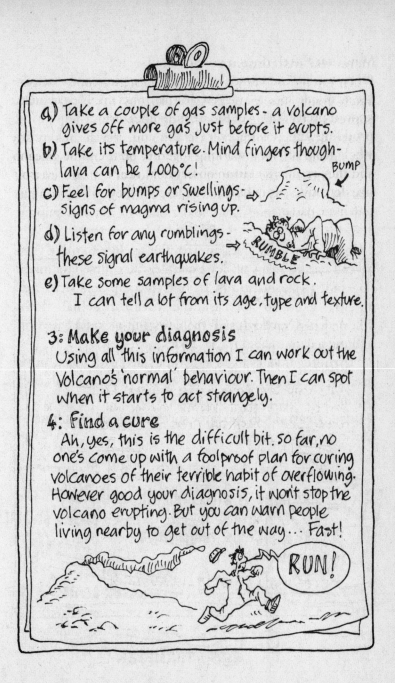

Incredible instruments

When you're working with volcanoes, a stethoscope won't do much good, but there is some serious machinery with impressive-sounding names that do help.

1 Satellite It's a lot bigger than the one that beams to the dish on the side of your house, and it can monitor ground movements on the volcano. It can detect a bulge even if magma's only rising by a few paltry centimetres. And it can map lava flows, mud-flows and clouds of ash and sulphur dioxide.

2 Computer This links up with the satellite to make what we call hazard maps of, for example, the course lava might flow in if a volcano erupts. In 1992–3 computers were used on Mt Etna to forecast the path of actual flows. Volcanologists couldn't stop the flows, but they did have time to build a dam to hold the lava back!

3 Tiltmeter It looks like a long tube filled with water, and is used for measuring ground movements from ground level. Accurate to hundredths of a millimetre.

4 Laser beam Does the same sort of thing as the tiltmeter, but works electronically.

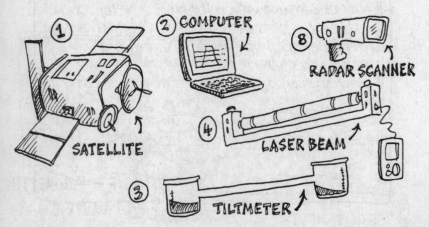

114

5 Seismograph (size-mo-graf) This measures earthquakes and can detect shock waves from movements deep below the Earth, which indicate that magma's rising.

6 A robot called Dante II This little chap is great for collecting gas samples, taking the temperature and making life a little easier for us, especially in the parts of volcanoes where even volcanologists dare not tread. He's armed with video cameras, too, so we can see exactly what's going on. Dante II was supposed to explore other planets but he proved so useful on Earth, that he never got off the ground.

7 Pyrometer This is a sort of thermometer for lava, it takes its temperature from a safe distance. You can use a thermocouple (electric thermometer), too.

8 Radar scanner Hand-held. For measuring the lava's speed. Originally used for catching speeding motorists!

9 Gas sampler Like a plastic tube attached to a bottle. You stick it in a fumarole. An erupting volcano can give off 100,000 tonnes of sulphur dioxide a day. (You could also keep a clothes peg in your pocket, too!)

10 Hot rod Long metal rod for collecting molten lava. You dip it in, twist it round and pull it out.

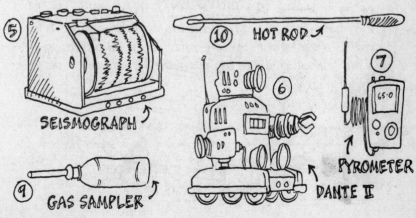

⑤ SEISMOGRAPH

⑩ HOT ROD

⑥ DANTE II

⑦ PYROMETER

⑨ GAS SAMPLER

Make your own volcano

If you don't have access to a volcano near you, why not make one of your own? That's what the makers of the film *Dante's Peak* did. The film tells the story of an active (but make-believe) volcano in the Cascade Mountains, USA. It is about to erupt, any minute. For the starring role, the film-makers built a 10-metre high model out of wood and steel, and wheeled it out of the studio whenever they needed it for a scene. Complete with computer-generated smoke, ash and lava!

Earth-shattering fact
In 1996, volcanologists in Italy made Mt Vesuvius erupt. On purpose! Why? They said they wanted to see what would happen. They dug 14 holes in the freaky peak's side, then dropped in loads of high explosives. These were blown up by a ship in the bay. BANG! By recording the incredible shock waves from the explosions, the scientists could see what was happening inside. 'We wanted to know what Vesuvius would be like if it woke up,' said one of the scientists. Weird!

Tragedy at Galeras

Volcanoes can be a bit like people. Just when you think you know them really well, they go and do something quite unexpected.

Violent volcanoes can be especially unpredictable. Just when you think you've got their number, they can blow up in your face. Several volcanologists are killed every year when the volcanoes they're studying erupt without warning. It's a horribly risky job. Take the tragic events at Galeras, for example.

On 14 January 1993, Galeras volcano in Colombia turned into a killer mountain. A VIP volcano, Galeras was being monitored by a team of volcanologists, led by American scientist, Professor Stan Williams. He had taken a party into the crater to collect gas samples. So far, so good. The volcano was active but had shown no signs of life for six months or so, and was, therefore, thought to be safe. Or safe enough. Then the unexpected happened. Without warning, the ground began to rumble and shake and, before the team could get out of harm's way, violent Galeras exploded. In a desperate attempt to save himself, Professor Williams started to run through a rain of rocks as big as TV sets. He didn't make it far. One flying rock broke his skull and jaw. Another smashed both of his legs. His clothes and backpack were set on fire. Slowly and painfully, he crawled inch by inch behind a large boulder and took shelter. Fifteen minutes later, the eruption stopped as suddenly as it began. But it was another two hours before Professor Williams was found, half-dead, and pulled to safety. Despite his horrible injuries, he had had a lucky escape. Three of his colleagues also survived. But six volcanologists and three tourists were killed outright by Galeras's sudden and savage fit of rage.

Professor Williams underwent months of surgery and eventually he was fit enough ... to visit the crater of Galeras again.

Some Earth-shattering facts about Galeras

1 Galeras is 4,270 metres high and lies just 6 kilometres from the busy city of Pasto in south-western Colombia. Pasto is home to some 300,000 people...

2 ...who are in grave danger if the volcano erupts, mainly from pyroclastic flows. For this reason, Galeras was picked as one of the world's 15 VIP volcanoes. It needed watching.

3 Galeras had been dormant until 1988 when it suddenly erupted. It is now classed as an active volcano.

4 Since then, volcanologists have kept a close eye on Galeras. A new observatory has been built and new instruments installed. In future eruptions, the earlier scientists can raise the alarm, the sooner Pasto can be evacuated.

5 Before the explosion, there were a few minor earthquakes but that was nothing to worry about. Two tiltmeters positioned on the volcano's side had showed no change. A fumarole had grown cooler, not hotter, and there was only the slightest trace of gas. Further proof that there was nothing to fear. But, with volcanoes, you never know...

118

6 Another lesson was learned the hard way. Only one of the group was wearing protective gear. It saved his life. Since then, volcanologists have been better prepared.

7 The volcanologists killed in the tragedy were taking part in an international workshop to study ash, rocks and other debris from past eruptions. They were totally dedicated to their work. Even with such a high price to pay.

Saving lives and false alarms

If volcanologists weren't prepared to risk their lives, then disasters could be even worse. Studying violent volcanoes can save lives. The more scientists know about volcanoes, the earlier they can warn of trouble. If they suspect a volcano is waking up, they can give the order to evacuate ... fast. Any delay could cost lives. Sounds straightforward. But it isn't. Some people don't listen to the scientists' warnings.

Then there's the question of getting it right. Even with the latest in high technology, scientists don't strike lucky every time. Sometimes it's a false alarm. But better to be safe than sorry, they say.

Getting it wrong

Things don't always go according to plan. When Nevado del Ruiz in Colombia erupted in November 1985, a lethal lahar completely demolished the nearby town of Armero. Almost 25,000 people died as waves of mud 40 metres high simply swept Armero away. Ten thousand more lost their homes. Although only a tenth as violent as the eruption of Mt St Helens, it was the greatest volcanic disaster of the century, second only to Mt Pelée in terms of lives lost. (About 29,000 people died when Mt Pelée blew.) The tragedy was, it needn't have been. Scientists warned the government officials what to expect. But they didn't take them seriously. They claimed they couldn't run the risk that it might turn out to be a false alarm. In the event, the eruption began at three p.m. on the afternoon of 13 November. By evening, despite a meeting of the emergency committee, no evacuation plans had been made. By the time they had been, it was too late. At nine p.m., Nevado del Ruiz began to belch out pyroclastic flows which melted part of its ice cap. A lethal lahar of water and ash raced downhill at speeds of up to 40 kilometres an hour. Two hours later, it hit Armero. It was too late for anyone to get out of its way.

Getting it right

Which makes getting it right even sweeter. When Mt Pinatubo in the Philippines erupted violently in 1991, scientific know-how saved thousands of lives. One of the biggest eruptions of the 20th century, it came right out of the blue – the volcano hadn't murmured in living memory. Ash, lahars and pyroclastic flows devastated the surrounding countryside. Tens of thousands of people lived on or near the volcano. Over a thousand died. And a million lost their homes and livelihood. But, believe it or not, it could have been worse. A whole lot worse. The scientists acted fast. At the first sign of trouble, they evacuated everyone living within 10 km of the summit. Then, using a network of portable seismographs, they monitored the volcano day and night. A hazard map showing possible danger zones was quickly drawn up. This time officials and public alike followed the scientists' early warnings that Pinatubo was about to erupt. A video was shown, explaining the dangers but without all the tedious technical terms. The video alone saved thousands of lives – at least people knew what to do. Even so, they only just made it. On 12 June, the evacuation zone was extended to 30 kilometres and 35,000 people were forced to flee their homes. Just in time. Three days later, on 15 June, at six a.m., Pinatubo blew apart. An eruption cloud 12 kilometres high spread out like a skirt around the volcano. Pyroclastic flows snaked 16 kilometres from the summit. Lahars spilled over and covered the countryside. But, at least the volcano doctors had got it right.

Even so, they can't take all the credit. In fact, the first inkling scientists had that Pinatubo was stirring came from a passing nun. She walked into the Philippine Institute of Volcanology and told the stunned scientists the volcano was smoking! And she was right!

Today, predicting volcanoes is getting easier all the time. But it's still not an exact science. Violent volcanoes are horribly mysterious. And constantly changing. Which proves a real headache for the steamed-up scientists. Is the volcano about to blow? Or not? Should they order an evacuation? Or not? What if the volcano's calling their bluff? And many, many more vexing questions besides. And even if you can predict an eruption, there's nothing you can do to stop it. Absolutely nothing at all.

NOT-SO-VIOLENT VOLCANOES?

Like them or loathe them, violent volcanoes are here to stay. We'll just have to learn to live with them. And everyone or everything has their good points. Don't they? Even violent volcanoes. OK, so you wouldn't want one in your back garden (like poor Farmer Pulido and peaky Paricutin). But they do have their uses.

MAKING TOAST? WARMING YOUR SLIPPERS? BOILING AN EGG?

Here are some of the things you wouldn't have if there weren't any violent volcanoes.

Without violent volcanoes, you'd miss out on...

1 The odious oceans Believe it or not, it was violent volcanoes which created the oceans and seas. To find out how, you need to travel back in time some 4,600 million years to the early days on Earth. Things looked very different then. Our brand-new planet was covered with thousands of volcanoes. Which never slept. As they erupted, they shot out streams of water vapour, a steamy gas. This cooled and formed storm clouds, full of rain. The rain fell, filled the oceans and hey presto! Water also gushed up from underground. The oceans, however, weren't like the salty seas we know today. They were boiling hot, awesomely acidic and full of colourful chemicals. Not exactly the perfect holiday spot.

2 The awesome atmosphere The early Earth was an eerie place. For one thing, it had no atmosphere. Violent volcanoes changed all that. Over millions of years, they belched out gases – mostly steamy water vapour, colourless carbon dioxide and stinky sulphur dioxide.

It wasn't an atmosphere as we know it. For one thing, you couldn't have breathed it in – it didn't have any oxygen. (This had to wait for plants to come along. They release oxygen when they make their food. But that's another story...) But it was certainly better than nothing.

3 Life itself That's about as useful as you can get. To tell the truth, volcanoes didn't actually create life themselves. But they created the right conditions for it. Life is thought to have begun in the odiously early oceans. The first living things were tiny bacteria which grew about 3,200 million years ago. How do we know? Scientists have found fossils of some of them in ancient rocks. They didn't need oxygen to live (there wasn't any, so it was just as well). Instead, they gobbled up chemicals from the hot soupy seas, especially nitrogen and sulphur which came out of violent volcanoes. A German scientist, who dedicated his life to studying weird wildlife, claims their descendants are still alive and well. They thrive around hot volcanic springs and volcanic vents in the sea floor. They also live in pools of oil, sulphur springs and rubbish heaps. As long as it's hot, steaming and smells terrible, they feel at home!

4 Monster mountains Some of the greatest mountains on Earth were built by violent volcanoes. Take the awesome Andes, for example. They run for more than 7,000 kilometres along the west coast of South America – the longest mountain chain in the world. This is where one plate (the one that carries the Pacific Ocean) is dipping under another (the one that carries South America). As the lower plate plunges down, it gets horribly hot and starts to melt. Then the molten magma rises up through the upper plate, triggering off violent volcanoes.

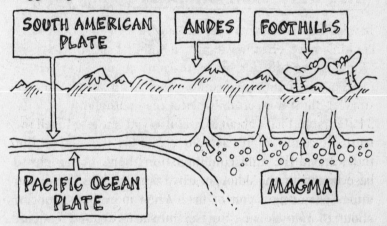

5 Flaming islands Many islands are in fact volcanoes – Iceland, Hawaii, Tristan da Cunha, the gorgeous Galapagos to name a few. They're actually the tips of underwater volcanoes, which have grown tall enough to keep their heads above water. There are thousands of volcanoes under the sea, all at least one kilometre tall. They've been built up over millions of years by lava creeping up through the crust. And they're still growing. As this story shows...

Happy birthday, Surtsey

No one had ever seen a volcanic island grow. That is, until November 1963. Then, early one morning, some fishermen off the coast of Iceland had the greatest surprise of their lives. As they watched, the sea began to smoke and steam, hissing like a kettle. At first, the fishermen thought a boat had caught fire. But when they got closer, they saw that the sea itself was boiling and bubbling. A violent volcano was coming up for air!

By next day, an island had been born. After they'd recovered from the shock, nearby islanders called it Surtsey, after their ancient god of fire. When it stopped erupting about 18 months later, Surtsey measured about 2.5 square metres, about as big as 100 football pitches. It was bare and black. But not for long. Within just a few months, the first plants began to grow from seeds carried there by birds or the wind. More seeds, and birds, followed. Four years later, the island was thriving.

Over a hot spot under the Pacific, not far from Hawaii, a brand-new island is starting to grow. Called Loihi, it's already 2,700 metres tall. Only another 1,000 metres to go until it pokes up out of the sea. Hawaii's actually a chain of 100 volcanoes. Some have now sunk back beneath the waves. Little Loihi will be the youngest in the family (ages range from an ancient 80 million years old to a measly one million years old). Scientists are already getting horribly excited and are keeping a very close eye on Loihi, sending down cameras and submarines. They're in for a very long wait. It'll be at least another 60,000 years before Loihi pops its fiery head above the windswept waves.

And there's something else lurking beneath those waves, it's the one bit of Hawaii that isn't volcanic...

6 Collapsing coral An atoll is a tiny ring-shaped island constructed of coral around a deep blue lagoon. You'll find them in warm, tropical seas. Lovely! But what have they got to do with volcanoes? Here's what.

a) A VOLCANIC ISLAND POPS UP FROM THE SEA...

b) A CORAL REEF GROWS ROUND THE ISLAND...

c) THEN SLOWLY THE VOLCANO STARTS TO SINK...

d) ...LEAVING THE REEF BEHIND

The first person to work this out was the brilliant British scientist, Charles Darwin (1809–1892). (Darwin was famous for discovering that horrible humans are descended from apes.) At the time, it was only a guess. Over a hundred years later, a team of scientists on Bikini Atoll in the Pacific were studying the effects of an atom bomb test. They drilled some holes into the atoll and found that the coral was indeed resting on volcanic rock. Darwin had got it right.

7 Famous landmarks Many of the world's most famous landmarks are volcanic. Take the Giant's Causeway in Northern Ireland, for example. It's made of hundreds of huge, hexagonal blocks and pillars of basalt formed millions of years ago when a volcano cooled. (There are no active volcanoes in Ireland today.) It's called a causeway because some of the rocks look rather like stepping stones, stretching 13 kilometres along the coast. Legend says that it was once a pathway for giants popping over to Scotland for a visit.

A violent future?

Violent volcanoes have been around for a very long time. And they're not going to go away. So what on Earth does the future hold?

VIP volcanoes

At present, scientists are monitoring about 100 of the world's 550 active land volcanoes. Closely. Another 300 need careful watching. Fifteen VIP volcanoes have been singled out for special study. They're the freakiest peaks in the world. And the most urgent to understand. You might have heard of some of them before...

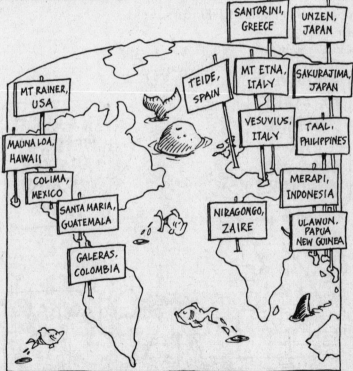

The modern world has never experienced a truly massive volcanic eruption. The last VEI 8 explosion was 75,000 years ago. But another one may soon be due. Horrible geographers reckon on two VEI 8s every 100,000 years. Some warn that a 'Big One' is already overdue. And it wouldn't be a pretty sight. The ashy aftermath of a really BIG explosion would blot out the Sun for years on end. No Sun means no plants which means NO FOOD. Now there's a horrible thought. So should we be worried? Are we living on borrowed time? What if the Big One happens soon? Before you start work on your volcano shelter, don't forget – 'soon' to a scientist doesn't mean today, tomorrow, or even next week, they're more likely talking 25,000 years away...

EARTH-SHATTERING EARTHQUAKES

INTRODUCTION

Geography can be shattering. But it's not the sort of shattered you feel after sitting through a double geography lesson. You know what I mean…

OF COURSE, ANY CLOSE INSPECTION OF THE LITHOSPHERE* WILL REVEAL THAT THE EARTH IS IN A CONSTANT STATE OF SEISMIC ACTIVITY**… BLAH! BLAH! BLAH!

I THINK MY BRAIN JUST BLEW A FUSE!

Z Z Z

* Lithosphere (Lith-ow-sfear) is the technical term for the Earth's crust. That's the bit of the Earth that you ride your bike on. It comes from an old Greek word for stone.

** Seismic (size-mick) is a tricky technical term for anything to do with earthquakes. It comes from an ancient Greek word meaning "to shake". A pretty accurate way of sizing up earthquakes, I'd say.

What on Earth is your geography teacher talking about? Roughly translated, he's saying that you're on very shaky ground. Simple, really.

WHAT HAPPENED?

I FELL OFF MY BIKE AND HIT MY ARM ON THE LITHOSPHERE

SEISMIC!

133

No, this sort of shattered is horribly different. Shockingly different, in fact. This sort of shattering splits the stony old Earth apart at the seams and turns people's lives upside down. So what causes this deadly devastation? An earth-shattering earthquake, that's what. And it makes double geography look like the best fun you've had in years.

The closest you'll ever get to an awesome earthquake is reading this book. YOU HOPE. But if you want to know what an earthquake might feel like, picture this scene...

One minute, you're snugly tucked up in bed, snoring and fast asleep. The next, your room starts shaking violently. Suddenly, you're flung out of bed and land with a crash on the floor. Shakily, you open one eye, then the other eye. It's chaos. There are books and clothes and mess everywhere. It feels like your world's fallen apart. And what on Earth is that terrible wailing sound? No wonder you're a quivering wreck. DON'T PANIC. Your house hasn't really been hit by an earthquake. It's just your mum stomping up stairs to drag you out of bed. (And she's yelling at you to tidy your room. Again.) It's a terrifying experience, I know, but you'll soon get over the shock.

And that's what this book is all about. Strong enough to shake a city to the ground in just a few seconds, deadly enough to smash the Earth apart, and more devastating than a nuclear bomb, earthquakes are the most shattering forces of nature ever. In *Earth-shattering Earthquakes*, you can...

- find out how on Earth earthquakes happen.
- learn how to spot the shocking warning signs.

- build a quake-proof skyscraper that won't fall down.
- try to predict a tremor with Sid, a seismologist*.

*That's a scientist who studies earthquakes. If you want to shake things up a bit, stick with me!

This is geography like never before. And it'll have you quaking in your boots.

A SHOCKING TRUE STORY

It was early in the morning on Wednesday, 18 April 1906. The city of San Francisco, the Pride of the West, lay slumbering in the darkness. Soon dawn would break over the sleeping city and the morning mist would give way to another beautiful day. Soon San Francisco would transform itself into a bustling city of half a million people, going to school and work. But for now, most people's curtains and blinds were still drawn. Some early risers were beginning to stir. Cable car drivers, factory workers and dockers on the early shift yawned, stretched and rubbed the sleep from their eyes. Time to get up and get ready for work. Just like any other day.

And then all hell broke loose...

At 5.13 a.m., without any warning at all, the earth beneath San Francisco gave a sudden, sickening lurch. For 40 earth-shattering seconds, the Earth shook the city to its core. Then there was a 10-second pause, followed by another massive shock. An angry, ominous, rumbling roar rose menacingly from the ground. Then the city was plunged into chaos.

It was early morning. The streets were deserted, apart from the milkmen on their rounds, and a policeman on his beat. Police Sergeant Jesse Cook saw the earthquake tearing down the street towards him.

"The whole street was undulating," he said. "It was as if the waves of the ocean were coming towards me, and billowing as they came."

Elsewhere in the city, the famous Italian opera singer, Enrico Caruso, was staying at the luxurious Palace Hotel, after a sell-out performance in the city's Opera House the evening before.

"Everything in the room was going round and round," he said, later. "The chandelier was trying to touch the ceiling and the chairs were all chasing each other. Crash! Crash! Crash! It was a terrible scene. Everywhere the walls were falling and clouds of dust were rising. My God, I thought it would never stop!"

Across the city, the shock sent buildings "reeling and tumbling like playthings". Glass and windows shattered into thousands of pieces. Pictures tumbled from cracked walls. Roadways buckled and heaved. Eerily, all the church bells in the city began to ring out at once. It sounded, one witness said, like the end of the world. Terrified people, shaken screaming from their beds, rushed into the streets, still in their nightwear. In their rush, they grabbed whatever they could. Some carried pet parrots or canaries, squawking in their cages. One man was seen wearing three hats. They were all he could find. Another man clung to a coal scuttle as though it was the most precious thing in the world. Other people wandered through the streets, or sat silently on the pavements. They were too shocked to cry, or even speak. No one could believe what had happened. They had never seen such devastation before. Not surprisingly. For that April morning San Francisco was struck by one of the deadliest earthquakes ever known.

As the rumbling stopped and the earth became still again, people tried to take stock. A heart-breaking sight met their eyes. Whole districts of the city had simply collapsed, or sunk into the ground. Almost every building in the downtown part of the city had been destroyed. Hundreds of people had been crushed to death under the falling rubble, and many more were badly injured. Some could be heard crying out from the shattered ruins. Then, just as it seemed things couldn't get any worse, things got worse. It was about 10 a.m., five hours after the first terrible tremor. Thinking the worst was over, a woman started cooking bacon and eggs for breakfast. She lit a match and threw it on to the fire. Then she watched in horror... The chimney had been damaged by the shaking and the fire set the roof of the kitchen alight. Within seconds, the whole wooden house had gone up in flames. The flames spread like wildfire to the rest of the block, then to the rest of the city. Unless something could be done, and fast, San Francisco would burn to the ground.

The city's brave firefighters rushed to the scene. They fixed their hoses to the nearest water pipe and waited for the water to flow. A thin trickle of water spurted out, then nothing... What on Earth was going on? Then they made a dreadful discovery. The earthquake had shattered the city's water mains and 300 million litres of water was slowly but surely leaking away, into the ground. With no water to use, the firefighters were helpless to put out the fire. All they could do was watch as the city went up in flames. San Francisco was doomed.

From their makeshift camps in the hills, thousands of people who'd escaped from the city also watched it burn. One shell-shocked eyewitness later wrote:

A sea of liquid fire lay beneath us. The sky above us seemed to burn at white heat, deepening into gold and orange and spreading into a fierce glare. The smoke had gathered into one gigantic cloud that hung motionless, sharply outlined against a vast field of exquisite starry blue... As night fell, it grew cold, and men and women walked up and down between the lines of sleepers, stretching their stiff limbs. Eyes, bloodshot from weariness and the pain from the constant rain of cinders, tried to turn away from the fire, but it held them in a dreadful fascination.

Fanned by fierce winds, the fateful fire blazed for three days and two nights. Then, on Saturday night, 21 April, at long, long last, it began to rain. Just in time. Next morning, the air was clear apart from dozens of wispy plumes of smoke rising from the smouldering ruins. All that was left of block after block of houses was charred, black remains. The city was unrecognizable. What buildings were still left standing were ghostly, burned-out shells. Old San Francisco had gone for ever.

EARTH-SHATTERING FACT FILE

LOCATION: San Francisco, USA

DATE: 18 April 1906

TIME: 5.13 a.m.

LENGTH OF SHOCK: 65 seconds

MAGNITUDE*: 8.3

DEATHS: 700

THE SHOCKING FACTS:

• The quake was the deadliest ever to strike the USA. Two thirds of the city was wiped out. Some 28,000 buildings were destroyed including 80 churches and 30 schools. About 300,000 people were left homeless.

• The city shook because it lay near the San Andreas Fault, a ghastly gash in the Earth's surface. An earthquake deep underground ripped the fault apart.

• San Francisco has grown so much that if such an enormous earthquake struck the city today, it could kill thousands of people and cause billions of dollars of damage.

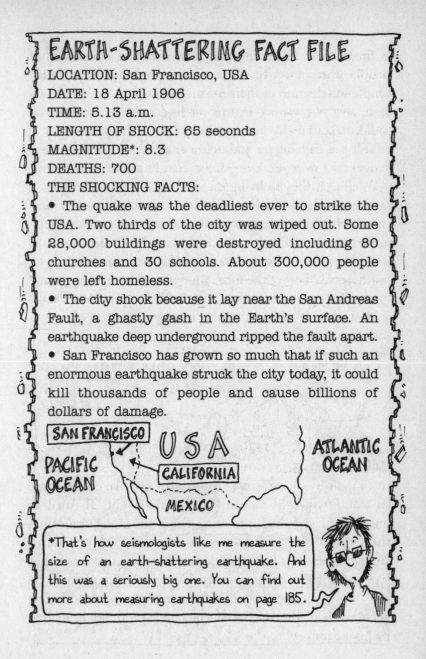

SAN FRANCISCO

USA

PACIFIC OCEAN

CALIFORNIA

MEXICO

ATLANTIC OCEAN

*That's how seismologists like me measure the size of an earth-shattering earthquake. And this was a seriously big one. You can find out more about measuring earthquakes on page 185.

In the nineteenth century, San Francisco had grown from a small village into a brand-new, booming city. No wonder people were proud of their town. And even though many of them lost everything in the earthquake, they knew they could make the city great again. In just a few years, they'd rebuilt the city, bigger and better than ever before. But the danger isn't over yet. Everyone in San Francisco knows only too well that they're living on very shaky ground. Another earthquake could strike anytime. The trouble is no one knows when. But what on Earth makes the seemingly rock-solid ground split apart at the seams? Where does the shocking force come from that can smash a city to smithereens? Forget the nice, tame bits of nature like pretty spring flowers and babbling brooks. This is geography at its wildest. And it's happening right beneath your feet... Are you ready to take the strain?

CRACKING UP

As the shell-shocked people of San Francisco found out, earthquakes are horribly unpredictable. You never know when one's about to strike next. The trouble is shaky quakes usually happen deep underground so it's shockingly hard to spot any warning signs. (Your geography teacher might have eyes in the back of his head but I bet even he can't see through solid rock.) For centuries, earthquakes were so mysterious that people made up stories about them to make sense of what was going on...

Shocking earthquake theories

1 The native people of North America thought a giant tortoise held up the Earth. Every time the touchy tortoise stamped its foot, it set off a gigantic earthquake.

2 In chilly Siberia, people believed the Earth was carried along on a giant sled, driven by a god called Tuli. Trouble was the dogs pulling the sled had fleas. When the flea-bitten muts stopped to scratch, it made the Earth shudder and shake.

I THINK IT'S TIME WE ALL HAD A BATH!

3 Some people in West Africa blamed a love-sick giant. The giant held up one side of the Earth, they believed, while a huge mountain propped up the other and the giant's wife held up the sky. When the soppy giant let his side go to give his wife a hug, guess what? Yep, the Earth shook.

4 In a Central American story, four gods held up the four corners of the Earth. When the Earth got too crowded, they simply shook one corner to tip some people off.

5 People in Mozambique, Africa, thought earthquakes happened when the Earth caught cold. Then you could feel it s-s-s-shaking with a terrible fever. Aaachoo!

6 According to Japanese legend, earthquakes are caused by a giant catfish which lives on the seabed. When the catfish sleeps (you could call this a catnap, ha! ha!), the Earth is nice and still. But when the fish wakes up and starts to wriggle, watch out. That's when you get an earthquake. (It must be a fantastically fidgety fish. Japan's one of the most earthquake-prone places on Earth.)

Could you catch a catfish out? Are you brave enough to save the world? To save the world from an earth-shattering experience, here's what you need to do.

What you need:
- a giant catfish
- a really large rock

What you do:

1 First, find your catfish. This might be easier said than done. The pesky catfish likes to bury itself up to its neck in mud, miles beneath the sea. And pack your suitcase – Japan's the best place to find this fish. Byeee!

2 Find a large (and I mean, *really* large) rock. You might need help with this bit. Do you *know* anyone crazy enough to help you catch a catfish?

3 Put the rock on the catfish's head so it's well and truly pinned to the seabed. Sounds cruel but the shaking should stop. Though you'll be faced with one angry old fish.

Notes:

If you feel weak at the knees just reading this, why not rope in a friendly god to help. The Japanese believed the gods were the only ones with enough power to keep the cranky catfish under control. It was only when the gods went on their holidays that the troublesome shaking began.

A bad case of wind

So, if you believe your legends, earthquakes are caused by a giant fish with a rock stuck on its head. Sounds like a very fishy story. What about any other crackpot theories? Well, there were plenty of those.

The Ancient Greek thinker, Aristotle (384–322 BC), had another earth-shattering idea. He blamed earthquakes on a bad case of ... wind. Yes, wind. Aristotle thought that earthquakes were caused by great gusts of wind gushing out from caves deep inside the Earth. Apparently, the caves sucked air in, heated it up, then blasted it out again. A bit like a gigantic, deafening fart. (Bet your teacher doesn't tell you this bit.)

But if fusty farts, crabby catfish and soppy giants weren't to blame, what on Earth was making the ground shake? Some religious leaders said earthquakes were God's way of punishing people for their sins. If people mended their wicked ways, the earthquakes would stop. Simple as that. (Whether or not it was true, it was a great way of making people behave better!) One old lady had other ideas. When an earthquake struck London in 1750, she thought it was caused by her servant falling out of bed.

Even horrible geographers got it wrong. In the 1760s, British geographer, John Michell, worked out (correctly) that the Earth shakes because of huge shock waves racing through the rocks. But he also thought (wrongly) that earthquakes were set off by the steam from enormous underground fires.

To tell you the truth, awful earthquakes had geographers stumped. And it might have stayed that way. Luckily, a brilliant German geographer, Alfred Wegener (1880–1930), was determined to get to the bottom of things once and for all. Even if it meant shaking things up a bit. This is his earth-shattering story…

Too much on his plate?

As a boy, Alfred Lothar Wegener spent much of his time staring into space. It drove his mother and father mad. They thought young Alfred was wasting his time and would never amount to much. But starry-eyed Alfred proved them wrong. He left school top of the class and went off to university to study astronomy (that's the posh term for learning about outer space). So all that star-gazing turned out to be useful after all. (Why not try this as an excuse next time your teacher catches you staring out of your classroom window?)

But even outer space wasn't enough for adventurous Alfred. His other great love was the weather. The stormier, the better. In 1906, he set off for Greenland to study wind. This might not be your cup of tea but Alfred liked it so much he went back again in 1912, 1929, and in 1930. And when he wasn't travelling, he taught meteorology (that's the posh name for studying the weather) and geography at university. Oh yes, Alfred was a real clever clogs.

But even when Alfred was busy teaching, his mind kept wandering to other things. (Does this ever happen to *your* geography teacher?) He really wanted to find out more about how the Earth works. At night, he used to hurry home and scribble his earth-moving ideas down in a notebook. Here's what it might have looked like...

My (top) secret notebook by Alfred Wegener

One day in 1910...
I'm SO excited, I could burst. It's this cracking idea I've had. It's been worrying away at me for weeks. It all started, you see, when I was showing some of my students where Greenland was on a map. (Call themselves geographers!) Anyway, I suddenly noticed something very strange. Get this. The east coast of South America looked like it fitted snugly into the west coast of Africa. Just like two pieces of a giant jigsaw! But how can that be? Before I get too carried away, I'm going to tear up some newspaper and test out my idea. (I've decided not to tell anyone else about it just yet. Just in case it doesn't work.)

Next day...
It works! It works! I tore up the newspaper, like I said. And guess what? The two bits fitted perfectly. It's amazing. You

can hardly see the joins. But there's a very long way to go. I mean, if the two continents were once joined up, how on Earth did they drift so far apart? I really hope I can crack the problem.

Some time later...
I've done it! I really think I've done it this time! And it's ground-breaking stuff, I can tell you. This is what I think has happened. By the way, I've based my ideas on my last Greenland trip when I was watching some icebergs drifting off out to sea. Fascinating things, icebergs. But that's another story. (Sorry the sketches aren't much good.)

1 About 200 million years ago, all the continents (including Africa and South America) were one massive chunk of land. I've called it Pangaea (that's Ancient Greek for "all lands"). I reckon it was surrounded by a huge sea.

2 About 150 million years ago, Pangaea split in two...

3 Then the two big pieces split into lots of smaller bits which began, ever so slowly, to drift apart... Millions and millions and

millions of years later, these bits ended up as the continents we have today (including Africa and South America). Brilliant, eh?

Note: I'm calling my new theory "continental drift". I know it's boring but it'll do for now. Annoyingly, I still can't work out exactly what gets the continents drifting. Never mind. Perhaps it's time to check out some more lovely icebergs.

Two years later...

I've been so busy giving talks about my theory that I haven't had any time for notes. If I'd known it'd be such a shaky ride, I'd have jolly well stuck to teaching. It's been pretty depressing, actually. The problem is no one believes me. No one at all. They say I've made the whole thing up and the whole thing's just coincidence. Pah! See if I care. I'll show them I'm right. If it's the last thing I do. And what's more I can prove it. Ready?

151

My proof

1 Mesosaurus was an ancient reptile that lived about 300 million years ago. These days it's extinct but get this, you only find its fossils in Africa and South America. This proves that the continents were once joined up and drifted apart later. I mean, how else would you find identical reptile remains in two different places, separated by thousands of kilometres of sea?

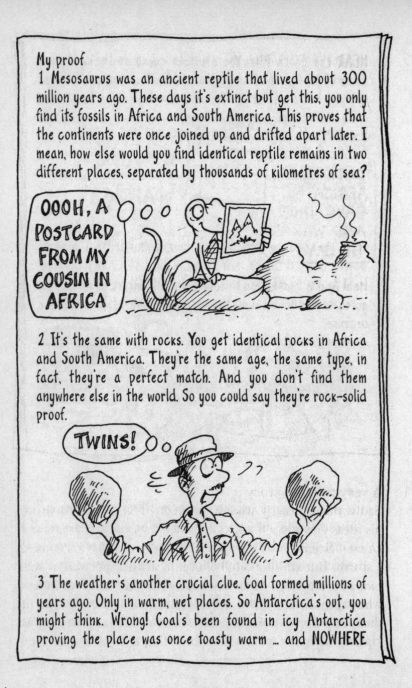

OOOH, A POSTCARD FROM MY COUSIN IN AFRICA

2 It's the same with rocks. You get identical rocks in Africa and South America. They're the same age, the same type, in fact, they're a perfect match. And you don't find them anywhere else in the world. So you could say they're rock-solid proof.

TWINS!

3 The weather's another crucial clue. Coal formed millions of years ago. Only in warm, wet places. So Antarctica's out, you might think. Wrong! Coal's been found in icy Antarctica proving the place was once toasty warm ... and NOWHERE

NEAR the South Pole. You also get the opposite happening. Some of the rocks in Africa and South America are covered in scratches, made years ago by ancient glaciers. So you see, once upon a time, these continents were a lot closer to the South Pole than they are today.

"LET'S GO TO AFRICA" HE SAYS, "NICE AND WARM" HE SAYS...

Hah! And if that doesn't prove I'm right, once and for all, I'm going to Greenland and I'm not coming back! And that's a promise.

MAYBE JUST ONE MORE SWEATER

A very moving story

Sadly, this is exactly what happened. In 1915, Alfred wrote his ideas down in a book, called *The Origin of Continents and Oceans*. Science was pretty stuffy then and the book caused a storm. But still nobody believed a word of it (well, it was *such* a boring title). Many top geologists (they're geographers who study rocks) dismissed his theory as rubbish. One of them called it "Utter, damned rot!" Another said Alfred was "taking liberties with our globe". (To tell the truth, they probably wished they'd thought up the idea themselves.) The main problem for Alfred was that he still couldn't work out what it was that made the continents drift. So he could prove things until he was blue in the face and it counted for nothing. Bitterly disappointed, in 1930 Alfred set off for Greenland. He was never seen again…

…which means he didn't live to see the day scientists finally believed his theory. For years after Alfred's death, his continental drift idea was completely forgotten. It wasn't until the 1960s that deep-sea scientists made a ground-breaking discovery that proved Alfred right. They found that some bits of the seabed are splitting apart, with red-hot runny rock oozing up through the cracks. When it hits the cold sea water, the hot rock cools, turns hard and builds massive underwater mountains and volcanoes. In other words, the seabed is spreading. But why doesn't the Earth get bigger as the seabed spreads? Where does all the extra rock go? Scientists soon found the answer. In other places, they found, one bit of seabed is being pushed down under the other. Then the rock melts back into the Earth. And guess what? The melting exactly balances out the spreading. This means the Earth always stays the same size. The seabed and the continents are all part of a hard, rocky layer around the Earth, called the Earth's crust. If one bit moves, it shoves the rest along too, as if it's on a colossal conveyor belt. So if the seabed is moving, the continents must be moving too. Alfred had been right all along. The continents are really drifting.

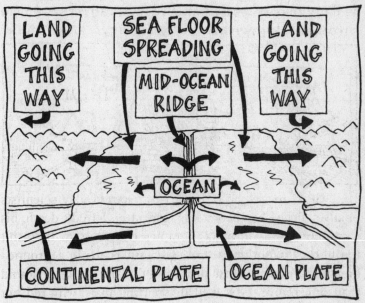

Scientists don't call this "continental drift" any more. They call it "plate tectonics" (teck-ton-iks, from the Ancient Greek word for building). They think this sounds much snappier. Do you?

What on Earth are earthquakes?

OK, you might say, but what on Earth does this have to do with earthquakes? Well, here's what else modern-day geographers have found out:

- The surface of the Earth (called the crust) is cracked into seven huge pieces called plates. (There are lots of smaller pieces, too.) Here's a helpful diagram:

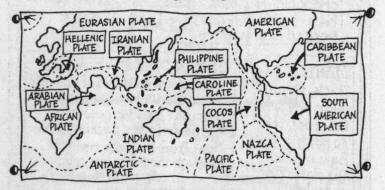

- But they're not the sort of plates you scoff your tea from. These are plates of solid rock which float on top of a layer of hot, bendy rock (called the mantle) – it's a bit like squidgy plasticine.

- Heat from the centre of the Earth (called the core) keeps the rocky plates on the move. (That's the bit that had poor Alfred stumped, remember?) You can't see all these layers from the surface. So here's an interesting X-ray view…

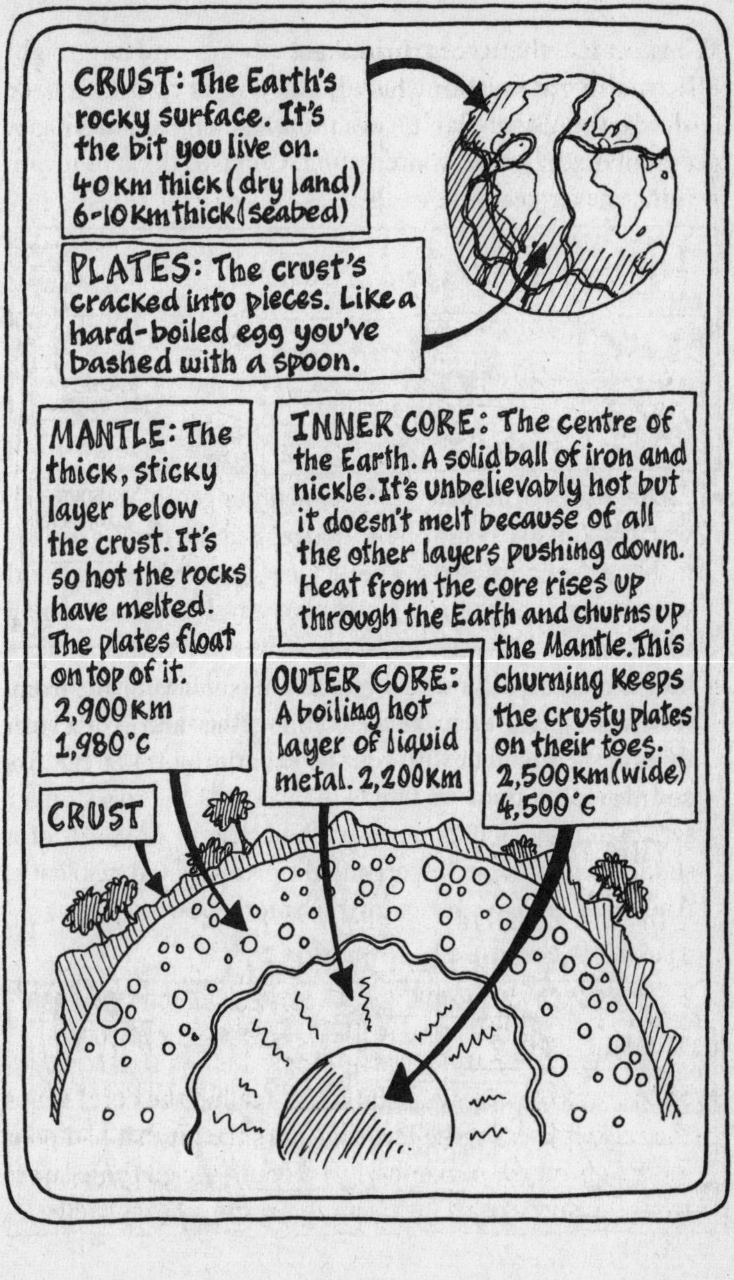

CRUST: The Earth's rocky surface. It's the bit you live on.
40 km thick (dry land)
6-10 km thick (seabed)

PLATES: The crust's cracked into pieces. Like a hard-boiled egg you've bashed with a spoon.

MANTLE: The thick, sticky layer below the crust. It's so hot the rocks have melted. The plates float on top of it.
2,900 km
1,980°C

INNER CORE: The centre of the Earth. A solid ball of iron and nickle. It's unbelievably hot but it doesn't melt because of all the other layers pushing down. Heat from the core rises up through the Earth and churns up the Mantle. This churning keeps the crusty plates on their toes.
2,500 km (wide)
4,500°C

OUTER CORE: A boiling hot layer of liquid metal. 2,200 km

CRUST

157

- The earth-shattering plates are always shifting, right beneath your feet. But luckily for you, they move so, so slowly, you usually can't feel a thing. Otherwise, walking to school might get very interesting. Come to think of it, you might never get there at all…

- As the plates drift along, they sometimes get in each other's way. It's a bit like being on the dodgems at the fair. As you try to barge your way past another car, you get bashed and scraped, until one of you has to give way. It's a similar thing with plates. They push and shove against each other, and get horribly jammed. (You could try this at home with two bits of sandpaper. Hold them sandy sides together and try to push them past each other with your hands. Any luck?) Over years and years, the pressure builds up and puts the rocks under serious strain. Sometime, something has to give. All of a sudden, the plates jerk apart and the ground shakes violently. And that's how you get an earth-shattering earthquake.

Earth-shattering fact
Thank your lucky stars you're not on the moon. Between 1969 and 1977 seismographs (size-mow-grafs)* picked up about 3,000 moonquakes a year. Most of the quakes were caused by meteorites (they're massive great lumps of space rock) smashing into the moon's surface. And if you're wondering how on Earth you find seismographs on the moon, they were left there by moon-walking astronauts.

* Seismographs are posh scientific instruments for measuring earthquakes.

Quick quake quiz

Is your seismic know-how all it's cracked up to be? Is it shockingly good or horribly shaky? Why not try this quick quake quiz to find out. If you've got enough on your plate (ha! ha!), try it out on your geography teacher. It'll have her quaking with fear.

1 How many earth tremors shake the Earth each year?
a) About 100.
b) At least one million.
c) About 10.

2 How long was the longest earthquake?
a) Four minutes.
b) One hour.
c) 30 seconds.

3 Where did the worst ever earthquake strike?
a) Japan.
b) China.
c) Italy.

4 How far away can you feel the shaking?
a) In the next town.
b) In the next country.
c) In the next continent.

5 How often do earthquakes shake Britain?
a) Never.
b) Not very often.
c) More often than you think.

Answers:

1b) Believe it or not, about one million earth tremors shake the Earth every year. That's about ONE EVERY 30 SECONDS. Luckily, most quakes aren't strong enough to rattle a tea cup. Only a few hundred really shake things up. And about 7-11 are truly earth-shattering.

2a) The awesome earthquake which struck Alaska in March 1964 lasted for four earth-shattering minutes. That's about the time it takes for you to get in from school, grab a can of pop, turn on the telly and veg out in your favourite armchair. No time at all really. But for the people who lived through this terrible ordeal, it must have felt like a lifetime. It was one of the strongest earthquakes known. Most earthquakes last for less than a minute. By the time you'd opened your pop, the shaking would be over. But in earthquake terms, even less than a minute is plenty long enough.

3b) Unfortunately, earthquakes are often rated by numbers of lives lost. And big quakes can be big killers. Experts estimate that 830,000 people died in the quake that struck Shaanxi, China, in January 1556. Making it the deadliest quake in history. Many people lived in caves carved out of the cliffs which crumbled apart around them. The deadliest quake of recent times was the one that struck Tangshan, China, in July 1976. It reduced the city to rubble. As many as 500,000 people lost their lives. A million more were injured.

4c) The colossal quake that hit Lisbon, Portugal, on 1 November 1755 was the worst European earthquake ever. The shaking was felt as far away as Hamburg and even the Cape Verde Islands – a massive 2,500 km away. It lasted for 6-7 minutes, which in earthquake time is a very long shake up!

5c) You're most likely to experience an earthquake if you live in California or Japan (check out the next chapter to find out why). But even Britain isn't totally tremor-free. Unbelievably, Britain has up to 300 or more earthquakes a year. Luckily, most are far too faint to feel. But not all of them. In April 1884, the people of Colchester in Essex got a nasty shock when a medium-sized earthquake shook the town, toppling several church spires and destroying 400 houses. In the villages near by, hundreds of chimney stacks tumbled down but nobody was killed. When a quake hit Shropshire in 1996 no one was hurt, but a hamster tumbled out of its cage. Poor thing!

IT'S A SHOCKING LIFE BEING A HAMSTER

Horrible Health Warning...

Earthquakes can seriously damage your health. Even though the Earth shook for less than an hour all together in the twentieth century, killer quakes caused more than two million deaths. DON'T PANIC. You're much more likely to be struck down by the flu. Still worried? Instead of sitting there shaking like a leaf, why not hurry along to the next earth-shattering chapter? It'll tell you where earthquakes are likely to happen so you know which places to avoid...

WHOSE FAULT IS IT?

Some places are deadlier than others. Take your geography classroom, for example. Think of all the horrors lurking behind that door. Geography books, geography tests, and worse still, geography teachers. Horrible. Now think of being on holiday. You're relaxing on a sandy beach after a dip in the warm, blue sea. (Where would *you* rather be?) It's the same with the stressed-out old Earth. Some places are barely bothered by earthquakes. Any tremors simply pass them by. Other places are on seriously shaky ground. A killer quake may be only seconds away. So where on Earth are these quake-prone zones?

Quick quake guide

Remember how the Earth's rocky crust is cracked into pieces called plates? Well, you'll find most of the shakiest places on Earth where two pushy plates meet up. In fact, this is how 95 per cent of all earthquakes happen. The exact type of earthquake you get depends on exactly how the plates behave. Feeling under pressure? Don't worry. Here's seismic Sid with his quick quake guide.

Hi, Sid here. Sizing up earthquakes is simple really. Once you know what you've got on your plate. Get two rock-hard plates together and something's got to give...

1 Pulling apart

In some places, you get two plates pulling apart. Red-hot, runny rock from the Earth's mantle oozes up to plug the gap. All that pulling sets off lots of small-ish earthquakes. Or you could call them seaquakes (well, they take place in the sea bed). Most of these quakes happen underwater, far from any land. So they're pretty harmless, unless, of course, you happen to be a fish…

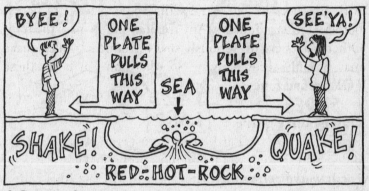

2 Going under

In some places, you get two plates crashing head-on in a colossal collision. One plate gets pushed under the other plate and its rocks melt back into the Earth. If you're planning a holiday near the coast, watch out. Slowly but surely, the seabed might be sinking under the land. Triggering off some of the worst earthquakes of all.

165

3 Slipping and sliding

In some places, you get two pushy plates trying to shove past each other. If they slide by nice and gently you get lots of tiny tremors. They're nothing to worry about and don't do much harm. But if one plate gives suddenly, beware. You could be in for a truly earth-shattering shock.

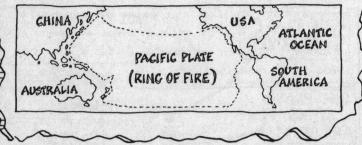

Earth-shattering fact

If you like living dangerously, why not hop in a boat and head off for the Pacific Ocean. It's lovely and warm and blue. But be careful. Deadly danger lurks in its depths. The land around the edges of the Pacific is the shakiest on Earth. This is where huge segments of seabed are sinking under the land, setting off massive earthquakes. In fact, three-quarters of all earthquakes happen here. Still going?

Teacher teaser

If you want to give your teacher a shock, put your hand up politely and ask him or her this harmless-sounding question:

> PLEASE, SIR, WHY DID THE MISSISSIPPI RIVER RUN BACKWARDS?

> ER... MISS, WHO?

Is this a trick question?

Answer: No, it isn't. In the winter of 1811–1812, the state of Missouri, USA, was struck by three of the worst earthquakes in American history. Each quake made the Earth shake more than 1,600 km away. And if that wasn't shocking enough, the quake caused the Mississippi River to change course completely and start to flow north instead of south. No wonder the fish were worried.

The fish weren't the only ones who got a nasty shock. The quake took everyone by surprise. You see, Missouri was the last place on Earth you'd expect to get an earthquake. It's nowhere near the edge of a plate. Seismologists now reckon that about five per cent of earthquakes happen in the middle of plates, probably along cracks left by ancient earthquakes. Trouble is, they don't know where these cracks are.

Finding fault

While your geography teacher's having her teabreak, knock on the staffroom door. Make up an excuse like, "Please, Miss, I want to be a seismologist when I leave school. Do I have to be good at geography?" While she's replying, sneak a good look at the mug she's using for her tea. Is it horribly chipped and cracked? Would one good tap shatter it into pieces? (Only try this if you *want* to do extra homework for the rest of your school days.)

Funnily enough, the stressed-out Earth is a bit like your teacher's old mug. How? Well, its surface is criss-crossed by millions of cracks.

The deepest cracks mark where two plates meet. Of course, horrible geographers don't call them cracks. They've thought up something much more boring. The tricky technical name is faults. But they're not the sort of faults your mum or dad mean when they tell you off for being untidy or picking your nose. These faults are weak spots in the Earth's crust, like the cracks in your teacher's mug. Pile on the pressure and these faulty rocks snap, triggering off earth-shattering earthquakes.

Geographers pick out three types of fault, depending on how the rocks move. Here are Sid's top tips for telling these fickle faults apart.

SID'S SEISMIC NOTE BOOK...

1 Normal fault. Watch out for places where two crusty plates are pulling apart. Tell-tale signs are where you see one slippery plate sliding under another.

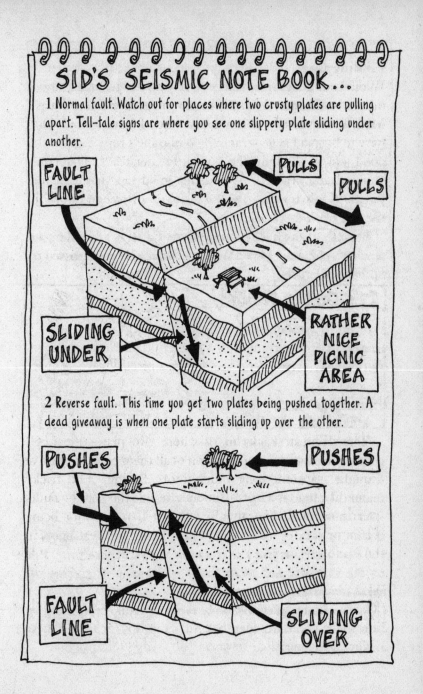

2 Reverse fault. This time you get two plates being pushed together. A dead giveaway is when one plate starts sliding up over the other.

3 Strike–slip fault. This is where two plates are sliding past each other. One slips one way. The other slips the other way. Very slippery characters. This means that fences or roads that once matched up don't match up any more.

WHAT HAPPENED TO THE ROAD?

SLIPS

SLIPS

FAULT LINE

Are you brave enough to pick fault in a fault?
To find out more about how strike-slip faults tick, why not try this tasty experiment. Go on, it's a piece of cake.

What you need:
- A cake (for the Earth's crust).
  Note: The best sort of cake to use is one with lots of layers of sponge, jam and cream. They'll look like the layers of rock in the Earth's crust. And they'll taste yummy, too.
- A knife. (Be careful.)

What you do:
1 Cut two large, gooey slices of cake.
2 Press the two slices together.
3 Now pull one slice towards you

170

and push the other away from you so they squidge by sideways. Congratulations! You've just demonstrated how a strike-slip fault works (well, almost). Simple, eh?

4 Now eat the bits of cake. Delicious!

P.S. Sick note: You can adapt this activity for the other two types of faults, too. But don't blame me if eating all that cake makes you feel horribly sick. If you do, that's your fault.

Faults – the shocking facts

1 The most famous fault on Earth snakes across sunny California, USA. Here the Earth's literally splitting apart at the seams. This crazy crack's called the San Andreas Fault and at any time now it could shake California to the core.

2 From the air, the fault looks like a ghastly scar running across the landscape. It's about 15–20 million years old and about 1,050 kilometres long, with lots of smaller faults running off it. No wonder California's feeling the strain. It suffers more than 20,000 tremors a year.

3 The fickle San Andreas Fault marks the place where the North American Plate (on the east) meets the Pacific Plate (on the west). It's a strike-slip fault (remember those?) which means the plates are sliding past each other. Actually, both plates are sliding in the same direction. But because the Pacific Plate moves much faster than the North American, it looks like they're pulling in opposite ways.

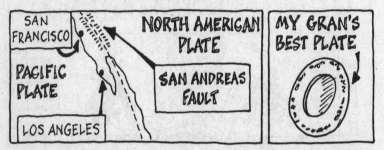

4 For most of the time, the plates slip by smoothly and trigger only tiny tremors. Creepy geographers call this creeping along. Sometimes, though, the plates get horribly jammed. The pressure builds up ... and up ... and up, until one plate gives way under the strain and the other plate jerks forwards.

5 You might think any sensible person would prefer to keep their feet on much firmer ground. But you'd be wrong. Horribly wrong. If mingling with famous film stars is your cup of tea, head for Los Angeles (the home of Hollywood). About 14.5 million people live in the city, perilously close to the San Andreas Fault. Another big city, San Francisco, sits practically on top of it. And, as you know, San Francisco's horribly earthquake prone. Remember the disastrous 1906 quake?

6 Seismologists say the most fragile bits of the fault are the north and south ends. They've been storing up trouble for centuries. And they could reach breaking point at any time ... with catastrophic consequences. As they've done many times before. Time to pay a second visit to shaky San Francisco…

The Daily Globe

18 October 1989, San Francisco, California, USA

CITY REELING FROM KILLER SHOCK

The stunned residents of San Francisco are still reeling from the shock today after yesterday's massive earthquake. Measuring 7.1 on the Richter Scale, it was the biggest quake to hit the city since the Great Quake of 1906. Once again, San Francisco has been shocked to the core.

The quake struck the city in the early evening, at the height of the rush hour. Thousands of people had already left work and were on their way home. The freeways were jammed with rush hour traffic. Pedestrians packed the pavements, chatting or stopping for a beer. At the Candle-stick Football Park, the game was already in full flow. The San Francisco

Giants were playing Oakland in the American Baseball World Series. Some 62,000 fans had packed the stadium to cheer their team on. All in all, just a normal day in the life of our busy city.

Then, at 5.04 p.m., disaster struck. In the Santa Cruz mountains to the south of the city, a section of the San Andreas Fault snapped suddenly under centuries of strain.

SNAP TO IT

A 40-kilometre crack ripped the Earth open. Just six short seconds later, the shock waves reached San Francisco...

For 15 seconds, the city was shaken to its core. Fifteen seconds that seemed like for ever.

SHAKY START

Reports just reaching us put the death toll at about 68 but with thousands more people injured or missing. All over the city, buildings have been toppled and smashed apart. A 1.5-kilometre stretch of the freeway has snapped in two and collapsed, crushing motorists underneath. Elsewhere in the city, thousands of homes and businesses lie in ruins.

The worst-hit parts of the city are those around the bay, which were built on land reclaimed from the sea. Here houses and apartment blocks have simply sunk into the soft ground.

With the risk of aftershocks a real possibility, the city's emergency services have lost no time clearing the streets. Their advice to everyone is to go home, turn off the gas (in case of fire) and stock up on food and bottled water.

HEAD HOME

Now the terrible task of rescuing the injured from the rubble can begin in earnest.

The clean-up of the city will take many years. Rebuilding people's shattered lives will take even longer. But most San Franciscans realize they have been lucky this time. They know it could have been worse. Much worse.

For some time now, seismologists have been predicting the Big One. No one knows if this was it. An even more powerful quake may be just round the corner. Despite everything, it's a risk many people are willing to take. Asked if she would now leave the city, one woman told us,

"Why should I? This is my home. Anyway, I survived the last one, didn't I? What are the chances of being in another?"

HOME SWEET HOME

Only time will tell…

EARTH-SHATTERING FACT FILE

LOCATION: San Francisco, USA

DATE: 17 October 1989

TIME: 5.04 p.m.

LENGTH OF SHOCK: 15 seconds

MAGNITUDE: 7.1

DEATHS: 68

THE SHOCKING FACTS:

• The city's major skyscrapers swayed by several metres but did not fall down. Still, the quake was horribly costly, causing almost $6 million (£4 million) of damage.

• In the year after the earthquake, more than 7,000 aftershocks were recorded around San Francisco. Five of them measured more than 5.0 on the Richter Scale.

• For such a big earthquake, the death toll was low. Thanks to the brilliant emergency services (fire, police and ambulance). In cities like San Francisco, the emergency services are trained to be ready and waiting when a quake strikes. An alarm sounds to give them a 20-second warning. It doesn't sound long but it's long enough to get rescuers and equipment in place, fast.

SAN FRANCISCO   USA   ATLANTIC OCEAN

PACIFIC OCEAN   CARIBBEAN SEA   SOUTH AMERICA

While you're still in shock, here's a warning about the next chapter. This book has got off to a very shaky start. But things are about to get worse. Feeling brave? You'll need to be as you wave goodbye to this earth-shattering chapter and crash into the next one…

Shattering Shock Waves

Picture another scene. This time you're not at home in bed. You're sitting in your classroom, snatching another quick snooze. Suddenly, the Earth starts to shake. You wake up with a start. The windows are rattling, your teeth are chattering, books and pencils are flying everywhere… What on Earth is going on? DON'T WORRY. It might feel like you've been struck by an earthquake but thankfully you haven't. It's only your geography teacher exploding with rage.

A real-life earthquake's a million times more mind-blowing. (If you can imagine that.) And, believe it or not, all this mayhem and chaos is down to a bunch of waves…

What on Earth are shock waves?
Forget the waves you see rippling across the sea. The sort that give you a soaking when you're swimming or capsize your canoe. These waves aren't wet or windswept. No wonder you're confused. Time to call in Sid, our expert…

WHAT ON EARTH ARE THESE WAVES, THEN, IF THEY'RE NOT WET?

They're gigantic waves of energy. Don't worry, I'll explain. For years and years, strain builds up in the rocks until, one day, they go snap. Like a gigantic Christmas cracker. Then where does all that pent-up energy go? It blasts out through the surrounding rocks in gigantic, wobbly waves, that's where. You can't see this sort of wave. In fact, you can't feel them ... until they hit the surface and give the Earth a really good shake.

WEIRD. WHAT ELSE SHOULD WE KNOW ABOUT THESE SHAKY WAVES?

Well, for a start, there are several different sorts. When they were discovered, geographers got horribly excited and gave the waves boring names. Pretty sad, eh? Want to know what the waves are called? Sure about that? OK, here goes...

179

1 Body waves. These waves travel through the Earth's insides until they reach the surface. There are two main types:

- *P waves*. These waves make the rocks squash and stretch, like a massive spring. You press the spring down, then ping! It springs back again. It's the same with the rocks. The P stands for primary because these pushy waves reach the surface first. Well, I warned you the names were boring.

- *S waves*. These waves race through the rocks in ripples, like when you hold the end of a rope and give it a good shake. The S stands for secondary because, guess what, they're the second to surface.

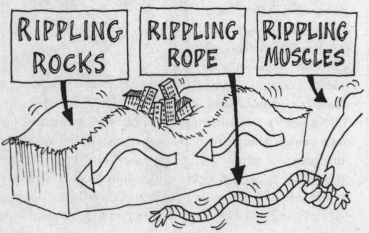

2 Surface waves. These waves shoot through the Earth's surface, shaking the ground up and down.

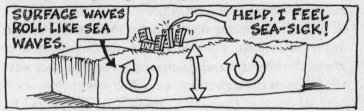

In the past, it was all the rage to name waves after horrible geographers. Now I know this doesn't sound very cool to you but the poor things considered it a great honour. Two of the most famous (waves and geographers) were called Love and Rayleigh.

- *Love waves.* After ace British geographer A. E. Love (1863-1940). He came across them while he was a professor of science at Oxford University. Love waves shift rocks from side to side.

- *Rayleigh waves.* After posh John Strutt, Lord Rayleigh (1842–1919). Lord Rayleigh was filthy rich and had his own private laboratory in his posh mansion. He was also a professor of physics at Cambridge University. Even though he'd been a sickly child, John was sickeningly brainy. He didn't have to go to school (how lucky can you get?). His rich dad hired a private tutor so he could do his

181

lessons at home instead. John loved science and maths (strange but true) and he also liked travelling. In fact, he had lots of his best ideas on holiday. Amongst other things, he worked out why the sky is blue and discovered a new gas in the atmosphere. For this, he won the Nobel Prize for Physics in 1904. He also discovered a type of surface wave which moves through rocks in a rolling action.

ROCK'N'ROLLIN' PROFESSOR

ROLLIN' ROCKS

HMM. BUT HOW DID THEY KNOW WHERE THE WAVES WERE, IF THEY COULDN'T SEE THEM?

Good point. You're smarter than you look. Actually, it was a mixture of using their imaginations and being brilliant at maths. First, they tried to imagine what the insides of the Earth looked like. Then they used maths to work out where the waves would be. Sounds like horribly hard work? Lucky I've brought a picture along...

AN EARTHQUAKE: the inside story

FOCUS: The spot underground where the rocks first go snap. It's also called the hypocentre. This is where the waves start from. It can be very deep down (over 300km); medium deep (300-70km) or shallow (less than 70km).

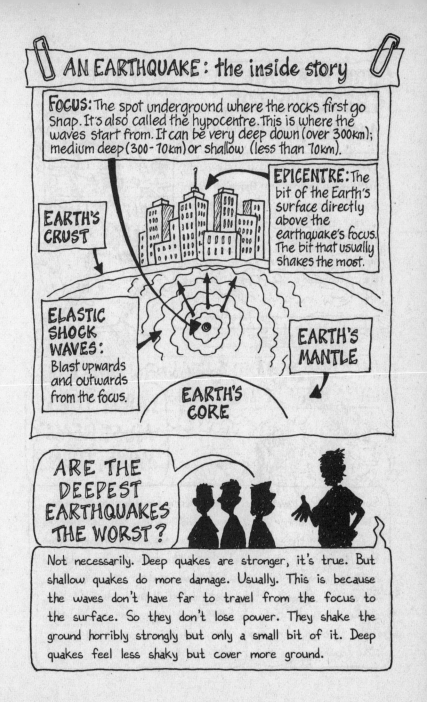

EPICENTRE: The bit of the Earth's surface directly above the earthquake's focus. The bit that usually shakes the most.

EARTH'S CRUST

ELASTIC SHOCK WAVES: Blast upwards and outwards from the focus.

EARTH'S MANTLE

EARTH'S CORE

ARE THE DEEPEST EARTHQUAKES THE WORST?

Not necessarily. Deep quakes are stronger, it's true. But shallow quakes do more damage. Usually. This is because the waves don't have far to travel from the focus to the surface. So they don't lose power. They shake the ground horribly strongly but only a small bit of it. Deep quakes feel less shaky but cover more ground.

HOW FAR CAN THESE WAY-OUT WAVES TRAVEL?

The waves from a seriously earth-shattering earthquake can travel thousands of kilometres around the Earth. Take the quake that hit Chile in 1960. The surface waves were so strong they whizzed 20 times around the Earth and could still be felt more than two days later.

WOW! THEY MUST REALLY MOVE, THEN?

Sure do. P waves (remember them?) are the fastest. They speed along at an awesomely quick six kilometres a second in the crust. That's like travelling from London to Paris in a minute! Ear-witnesses have reported hearing a loud roar as the waves hit the surface. S waves aren't far behind, followed by slower, surface waves. But the different types of rocks they race through can make the whizzy waves speed up or slow down.

Now you're a whizz with waves, you can put them to good use. Unlike Love and Rayleigh, seismologists don't have to guess what the Earth's insides look like anymore. They use shock waves to suss out about the rocks. They also use shock waves to work out just how horribly violent an earthquake is. Read on to find out more.

Scales of destruction

So how do you measure exactly how earth-shattering an earthquake is? It's shockingly difficult even for the experts. Why? Well, where on Earth do you start? With the earthquake's power? The damage it does? Or the size of the crack that caused it? In fact, geographers measure all three things. Which makes life horribly confusing. Here's Sid again to try to make sense of three of the handiest earthquake scales. Which one do you think works best?

A

Name: The Modified Mercalli Scale

What it measures: Earthquake intensity. This means how strongly the earthquake shakes the Earth and the damage it does. Records of earthquake intensity are great for studying ancient earthquakes. More importantly, they allow emergency services to be ready when an earthquake strikes. It's like listening to a rock band playing REALLY LOUD music… And they don't come much louder than the one, the only, the truly earth-shattering QUAAAKKES!

185

You can think of intensity as how loud the band sounds to your ears alone, no matter where you're standing in the concert hall – front, middle, back or even outside it.

THE DAMAGING DETAILS:

EARTHQUAKES ARE RATED ON A SCALE OF
I (1) TO XII (12). HERE'S HOW THE SCALE WORKS...

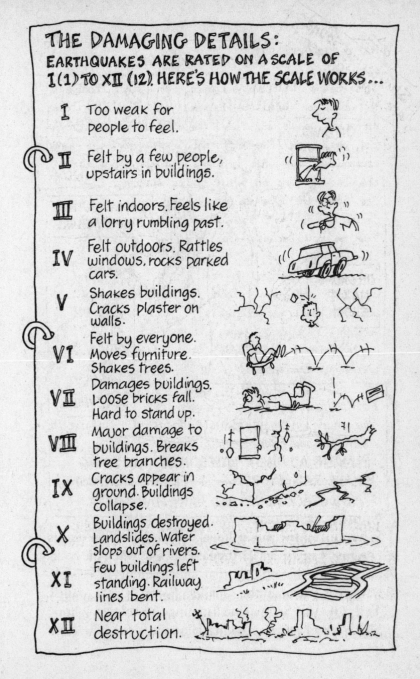

I   Too weak for
    people to feel.

II Felt by a few people,
    upstairs in buildings.

III Felt indoors. Feels like
    a lorry rumbling past.

IV Felt outdoors. Rattles
    windows, rocks parked
    cars.

V   Shakes buildings.
    Cracks plaster on
    walls.

VI Felt by everyone.
    Moves furniture.
    Shakes trees.

VII Damages buildings.
    Loose bricks fall.
    Hard to stand up.

VIII Major damage to
     buildings. Breaks
     tree branches.

IX Cracks appear in
    ground. Buildings
    collapse.

X   Buildings destroyed.
    Landslides. Water
    slops out of rivers.

XI Few buildings left
    standing. Railway
    lines bent.

XII Near total
    destruction.

What the experts say:

This scale's a bit hit and miss, I'm afraid. Trouble is it relies on what people see and feel. Ask five different people and they'll say five different things. So, you'd have five different grades for the same earthquake. See what I mean? And the intensity changes depending on where you're standing. (So when the Quakes played "Shake, rattle 'n' roll", it sounded really loud to you because you were standing right at the front. But your mate who turned up late and was stuck outside heard a quieter version.) Besides, who wants to hang around and check out the damage?

Earth-shattering fact
You can use anything to measure intensity. Even a horse. In Australia, some people compare the shaking felt in a slight earthquake to a horse scratching its back on a fence.

B

Name: The Richter Scale

What it measures: Earthquake magnitude. This means how much energy an earthquake releases when the rocks break. (It's this energy that shoots along in seismic waves.) Remember the Quakes? Sorry, REMEMBER THE QUAKES? Imagine listening to a solo on Johnny Shake's lead guitar. Making allowances for how close you're standing to the stage. So that it sounds just as LOUD wherever you are.

The damaging details:

The Richter Scale was named after top American seismologist Charles F. Richter (1900–1985). In 1935 Charles was put in charge of the Seismological Laboratory in a company called Caltech, in quake-prone California, USA. It was a plum job for a young man. But Charles wasn't bothered about fame and fortune. No. He was utterly fed up. Fed up with answering the phone all day to boring old journalists, asking the same boring old question,

You see, at that time, the only way of sizing up earthquakes was with the Modified Mercalli Scale. Trouble was, you never got the same answer twice. It was hopelessly unreliable. Grumpy Charles Richter scratched his head. He had to find something better. Something that even those pesky journalists could understand. Then Charles had a brainwave. He compared the time it took for the different waves to show up on his seismograph, to figure out how far away the earthquake was. Then he measured how far and how fast the ground was shaken about by the shock waves at the place where his seismograph was. Then, making allowances for how far away and how deep the earthquake was, he calculated how powerful it was. (Phew! It's complicated.) It was much more accurate and scientific. Charles's new, improved scale looked something like this:

0 - The tiniest tremors recorded

1 - Only felt by instruments

2 - Barely felt even near epicentre

3 - Felt near epicentre but little damage

4-5 - Felt further away. More damage

6 - Fairly destructive

7 - Major earthquake

hamster damage

8 - Great earthquake

And it doesn't stop there. Modern, ultra-sensitive seismographs can record really teeny tremors, down to –2 or –3. But don't think a magnitude 7 earthquake is only a little bit worse than a magnitude 6. On the Richter scale, each step up means a 10-fold increase. So a 7 is actually 10 times bigger than a 6 but only a tenth as big as an 8. Got it?

What the experts say:

> This scale's always a popular choice. It's the one they use on the telly. The only snag is it can't really cope with megaquakes. (They're the ones above 8.5.)

C

Name: The Moment Magnitude Scale

What it measures: Seismic moment. This measures the total size of an earthquake. The whole shocking lot. Meanwhile, back at the Quakes concert… Make allowances for how far you're standing from the stage. Then take out your earplugs and it's still like listening to the whole ear-splitting band, turned up really LOUD!

The damaging details:
This scale takes everything into account, from the first crack in the rocks, to how much the Earth shakes and how long the earthquake lasts.

What the experts say:

This scale is the experts' choice. It's tricky to calculate but awesomely accurate because it gives the whole earth-shattering picture. And it's brilliant for those really big quakes, between 9 and 10. So brilliant, in fact, that some of the biggest quakes have been upgraded. The 1960 Chile megaquake measured 8.5 on the Richter scale. Pretty big, you'd think. True, but actually it was much, much bigger than that. Its moment magnitude is now rated as 9.5, making it one of the most massive quakes ever.

Killer quakes
The catastrophic Chile quake was the most powerful quake of the twentieth century. But in the worst earthquakes ever, it doesn't even make the top ten. That's because many earthquake lists are based on the numbers of people killed. It's tragic but true. In Chile's case, some 2,000 people lost their lives. Which was pretty bad. But for such a great quake, it was amazing there were so many survivors.

TOP TEN EARTHQUAKES

	LOCATION	DATE	DEATHS	MAGNITUDE
10:	Chihli, China	1290	100,000	Unknown
9:	Kanto, Japan	1923	142,000	8·3
8:	Ardabil, Iran	893	150,000	Unknown
7:	Nan-Shan, China	1927	200,000	8·3
6:	Gansu, China	1920	200,000	8·2
5:	Damghan, Iran	856	200,000	Unknown
4:	Aleppo, Syria	1138	230,000	Unknown
3:	Tangshan, China	1976	242,000	7·9
2:	Calcutta, India	1737	300,000	Unknown
1:	Shaanxi, China	1556	830,000	8·3

NB: Some of these earthquakes were so long ago that experts have had to estimate their magnitude. But if they were big enough to go down in history, they must have been pretty bad!

Some of these quakes happened a long time ago when there weren't any accurate records. So the numbers of deaths are based on guesswork. The true numbers might be much higher ... or much lower. There's really no way of telling.

One thing's for certain. Earth-shattering earthquakes are horribly dangerous. And they can happen almost anywhere, at any time. So to be on the safe (well, safe-ish) side, surely it's best to stay away from places known to be prone to quakes? You'd think so, wouldn't you? You really would. But plenty of people would disagree...

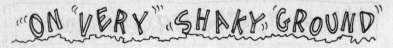

What do places like San Francisco, Los Angeles, Mexico City and Tokyo have in common? Give up? The answer is they're some of the biggest and busiest cities on Earth. And they're all built on very shaky ground. So why on Earth do people live in such horribly hazardous places? After all, a big quake could raze a big city to the ground in a matter of seconds. Amazingly, some 600 million people still live in quake-prone zones. Despite the appalling dangers. If you ask them why they don't just move out and go and live somewhere safer, they'll probably reply that for most of the time they're as safe as houses at home.

Besides, the worst may never happen. But then again, it just might...

Catastrophe in Kobe

Kobe is a bustling city in southern Japan. It's one of Japan's biggest ports and an important centre of industry. Unfortunately, earthquakes shake Japan regularly, though there hadn't been a big quake in Kobe for some time. Until 17 January 1995, that is. So what does it feel like when your world's shaken apart? Here's how the events of that fateful day might have appeared to a young boy.

194

the earthquake by yoshi

We learned all about earthquakes at
school. So I knew Japan got loads
of them. Sometimes we did
earthquake drills. But they were
pretty boring. Anyway I wasn't a
bit worried. Kobe's a really brilliant
place. I've lived here all my life. It's
really nice and safe. Besides, I didn't
really believe in earthquakes, anyway.
But I do now...

Last Tuesday, things got really scary. It was early in the
morning and I was fast asleep. Next thing I knew, I was
thrown out of bed on to the floor. The floor was shaking. But
that wasn't all. We live in a block of flats and it wasn't just
the floor shaking. The whole building was shaking. It was really
scary. It was dark and I didn't know what to do. I could see
things skidding across the floor. I guessed it must be my
bookcase and my bed. To make matters worse, there was a
terrible noise, like a monster roaring. I heard my mum calling
to me and my sister. Then my dad came into my bedroom with
a torch. He told me to go into the kitchen and get under the
kitchen table, like we'd been taught at school. I
wish I'd taken more notice. It was hard to
stand up and walk but I did what my
dad said and went to the kitchen. My
sister was crying and hugging my
mum. You see, she's only five. I was
scared too but I tried not to show it.
The shaking seemed to last for ever

195

and ever. Then, at last, it stopped. Mum and Dad held our hands tightly and we ran out of the flats into the street. Outside, things were really bad. It was just getting light so we could see all the damage. Our building wasn't too badly hit but the block next door had toppled over and smashed to smithereens. It was the same all the way down our street. Half the houses had collapsed. It took a bit of getting used to. You think people's houses will last for ever. Some of them were my friends' houses. I really hoped they were safe. And there were these huge cracks in the pavement. Everything was ruined. One man said it was like a giant had stamped on the city and squashed it flat.

I sat on the pavement with my mum and my sister while my dad went to see if he could help. There were lots of people just sitting there, staring. My mum said it must be the shock. Anyway, I wasn't even frightened anymore. I was just sad and I was really cold. We left our house in such a rush we didn't bring our coats or anything with us. At least my mum and dad and sister are safe. Our next-door neighbour was trapped in the rubble and my dad helped pull her out. I was really proud of him. But there were lots of people shouting and crying because they couldn't find their friends and relatives. It was really horrible.

I don't know how long we waited in the street. It felt like hours. Then later that day, my dad fetched us and took us to a hall in another part of the city which wasn't so badly damaged. The hall belongs to the steel company my dad works for. Dad says his company will look after us for the time

being. We can't go home because there's no water or gas or electricity, and our house isn't safe. The hall's really noisy and crowded because there are lots of other families here.

But a man came and gave us some warm blankets and food. It was only rice-balls to eat but I was so hungry I didn't care. And it stopped my sister crying. Mum said that other people were staying in schools or shrines. And that all of us were the lucky ones. I'm glad we didn't have to stay in my school.

It's OK here and I've made some new friends but I don't know how long we'll be staying. Still, Dad says I must put a brave face on it and look after my little sister. I told him I'll try. But it isn't easy. Especially as Dad thinks we might be in for some aftershocks. They're little shocks after the big earthquake. I really, really hope he's wrong. I don't want to have anything to do with an earthquake ever again. I just want to go home.

EARTH-SHATTERING FACT FILE

DATE: 17 January 1995
LOCATION: Kobe, Japan
TIME: 5.46 a.m.
LENGTH OF SHOCK: 20 seconds
MAGNITUDE: 7.2
DEATHS: 4,500; 15,000 injured
THE SHOCKING FACTS:

• It was the deadliest quake to hit Japan since the Great Kanto Earthquake of 1923 when 142,000 people died.

• The quake caused massive destruction. Some 190,000 buildings were damaged even though many were meant to be earthquake-proof. Fire burned thousands more buildings down.

• The Hanshin Expressway, the raised main road linking Kobe to Osaka, keeled over on its side. Because it was early morning, the road was almost deserted. A few hours later and it would have been packed with cars.

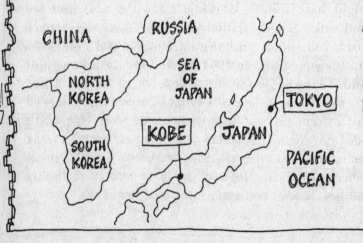

Seismic side effects

Smashing up cities seems shocking enough. But earthquakes have plenty of other nasty surprises in store. Here are some seismic side-effects you might want to steer clear of:

1 Earthquake ups and downs. Earth-shattering earthquakes can change the face of the landscape. So you might have trouble working out where you are. Some land sinks. Some's shoved up several metres into the air. Roads and railway lines that once met in the middle, don't meet anymore. In the 1964 Alaska earthquake, a chunk of land THE SIZE OF FRANCE tilted to one side. It left the fishing village of Cordova so far from the sea that the tide no longer reached the harbour! Leaving the fishermen's boats high and dry. Other normally dry places were flooded.

199

2 Lethal landslides.
On 31 May 1970, an
earthquake measuring 7.8
on the Richter scale shook
Peru. But worse was to come.
The earthquake triggered off a lethal
landslide on Mount Huascaran. It sent
millions of tonnes of rock and ice hurtling
downhill at devastating speed. The landslide
flung boulders and mud into the air and
pulverized everything in its path. Including the
town of Yungay. Within seconds, the town was smashed
to pieces and the townspeople were buried alive.
Altogether, on that one dreadful day, about 60,000 people died.

3 Flaming fires. Without doubt, the most sinister side-effects of earthquakes are flaming fires. Often fire does far more damage than the quake itself. Remember the woman cooking bacon and eggs in San Francisco? The combination of fire and mostly wooden houses turned breakfast into a nightmare. Another tragic case was the city of Lisbon in Portugal. In November 1755, an awesome earthquake hit the city. With devastating results. Large parts of the city lay in ruins. But worse, much worse, was to come. Within a few hours, sparks from overturned cooking stoves and oil lamps had lit a ferocious fire. For three terrible days, the fire swept through the city before, finally, burning itself out. Before the earthquake, Lisbon had been a beautiful place, filled with palaces, fine houses and priceless works of art. Afterwards, it was burned to a crisp. Luckily (for us), the fire was witnessed first hand by a man called Thomas Chase, an Englishman living in Lisbon. Here's what his letter home might have looked like:

Lisbon, Portugal
November 1755

Dearest Mother,

I hope this letter reaches you safely. The post isn't working too well these days. In fact, nothing's working in Lisbon at present. That wretched earthquake's turned our lives upside down. There's not much of the city left. Anyway, I wanted to let you know I'm safe. I'm one of the lucky ones.

I was in my bedroom when the ground started shaking. And there was the most dreadful sound I've ever heard. I knew at once that it was an earthquake. It was gentle at first, then it got stronger and stronger. I'm afraid curiosity got the better of me and I ran to the top of the house for a better look. (I know what you're thinking. Stupid boy! And you're right.) I'd nearly made it when the whole house suddenly lurched sideways and knocked me off my feet. Then I felt myself falling. In fact, I'd been thrown out of a window. (Unfortunately, it was on the fourth floor.) I must have passed out because the next thing I remember was my neighbour dragging me out from under a pile of bricks and rubble. He didn't recognize me at first, I looked such a sight.

Anyway, I was pretty shaken up, I can tell you. My poor body was covered in cuts and bruises, and I'd broken my right arm. (I'm afraid that's why my writing's so shaky.) Someone went and fetched my good friend, Mr Forg, and he took me to his house and put me to bed to recover. At last I was safe. Or so I thought. From my bed, I could spy yellow lights flickering outside the window and I could hear the sickening crackle of flames. Would you believe it, the house was on fire! Brave Mr Forg acted quickly. Twice now he's saved my life. At great personal peril, he carried me to safety in the Square, and there I stayed all Saturday night and Sunday. By now, the whole city was on fire. I wept to see it burning out of control.

As I said, dear Mother, despite my wounds, I was lucky. Although I've lost everything, I still have my life. Many of my friends are much worse off. It has been terrible. Terrible.

Anyway, I'll write again soon. And I may see you even sooner. As soon as I'm better, I'm coming home. Until then, please don't worry about me.

Your loving son,
Thomas

excuse thumbprint →

X X X X X

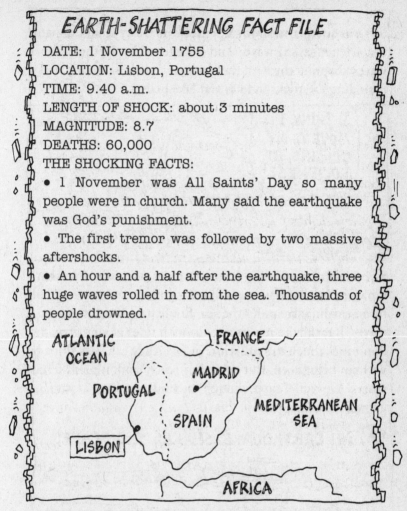

EARTH-SHATTERING FACT FILE

DATE: 1 November 1755
LOCATION: Lisbon, Portugal
TIME: 9.40 a.m.
LENGTH OF SHOCK: about 3 minutes
MAGNITUDE: 8.7
DEATHS: 60,000
THE SHOCKING FACTS:

• 1 November was All Saints' Day so many people were in church. Many said the earthquake was God's punishment.

• The first tremor was followed by two massive aftershocks.

• An hour and a half after the earthquake, three huge waves rolled in from the sea. Thousands of people drowned.

ATLANTIC OCEAN

FRANCE

PORTUGAL

MADRID

SPAIN

MEDITERRANEAN SEA

LISBON

AFRICA

4 Shocking seiches. Spare a thought for the locals who lived around Loch Lochmond in Scotland. They didn't know there'd been an earthquake in Lisbon. (It took two weeks for Britain to get the news.) So when the loch water suddenly started sloshing violently to and fro, they'd absolutely no idea why. What on Earth was going on? Well, this was another seismic side-effect. Its tricky technical name is a seiche (saysh) wave. And it's caused by all those shock waves shooting through the Earth and shaking up the rocks, including the rocks in loch and lake beds.

5 Terrible tsunamis (soo-naa-mees). A tsunami (that's Japanese for "harbour wave") is a gigantic wave triggered off by an earthquake under the sea. Some people call them tidal waves, but they're nothing to do with tides at all. Tsunamis don't look much to start with. In fact, they can pass ships by without being seen. But once they reach land, it's a different story. Are you brave enough to find out how a tsunami grows? What happens is this:

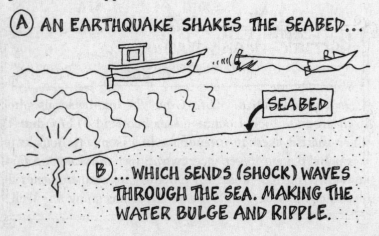

Ⓐ AN EARTHQUAKE SHAKES THE SEABED...

SEABED

Ⓑ ...WHICH SENDS (SHOCK) WAVES THROUGH THE SEA. MAKING THE WATER BULGE AND RIPPLE.

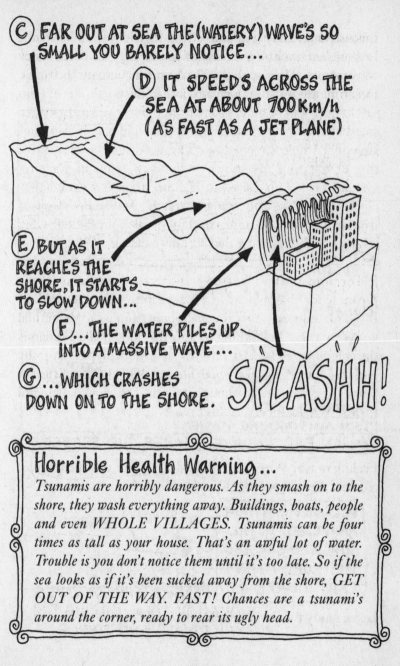

© FAR OUT AT SEA THE (WATERY) WAVE'S SO SMALL YOU BARELY NOTICE...

Ⓓ IT SPEEDS ACROSS THE SEA AT ABOUT 700 km/h (AS FAST AS A JET PLANE)

Ⓔ BUT AS IT REACHES THE SHORE, IT STARTS TO SLOW DOWN...

Ⓕ ...THE WATER PILES UP INTO A MASSIVE WAVE...

Ⓖ ...WHICH CRASHES DOWN ON TO THE SHORE.

SPLASHH!

Horrible Health Warning...

Tsunamis are horribly dangerous. As they smash on to the shore, they wash everything away. Buildings, boats, people and even WHOLE VILLAGES. Tsunamis can be four times as tall as your house. That's an awful lot of water. Trouble is you don't notice them until it's too late. So if the sea looks as if it's been sucked away from the shore, GET OUT OF THE WAY. FAST! Chances are a tsunami's around the corner, ready to rear its ugly head.

Life-saving early warning

In 1946, a tremor off the coast of Alaska triggered off a series of tsunamis. They sped 3,000 kilometres across the Pacific Ocean all the way to Hawaii. People in the port town of Hilo saw a sheer wall of water rising from the sea. Wave after wave smashed into the harbour, hurling boats and people aside and sweeping whole streets away. The good news is that, after this devastating disaster, a brand-new tsunami warning system was set up. Based in Hawaii, it keeps a round-the-clock earthquake and tsunami watch. At the first sign of trouble, it flashes warnings to stations all around the Pacific, telling people how long they've got to get out of the way…

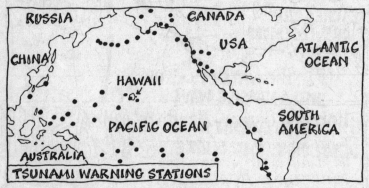

Teacher teaser

Feeling brave? Why not try this sick joke on your geography teacher? Put up your hand and ask:

PLEASE, MISS, WHAT HAPPENED TO THE COW WHO CROSSED THE ROAD IN AN EARTHQUAKE?

Is she ready for the side-splitting reply?

WHAT THE...

Horrible (Human) Health Warning

Forget crusty plates and restless rocks. Anything that puts the Earth under pressure can trigger off a shock. INCLUDING HORRIBLE HUMANS. One of the worst things humans are doing is filling reservoirs with water. (Reservoirs are like big lakes. They're sometimes used for storing drinking water.) So how on Earth does this set off an earthquake? Well, the weight of the water puts the rocks under serious strain, forcing water down into faults that are already there. In 1967, a massive 6.5 shock hit Koyna in India. The area wasn't known for earthquakes. But, guess what? A brand-new reservoir had just been filled up there.

In future, the numbers of people living on shaky ground is likely to go up and up. After all, quake zones cover large parts of the Earth and you can't avoid them all. Besides, shaking aside, they're often pretty pleasant places to live. So what can be done to make life safer? Time to call the earth-shattering experts in…

EARTH-
SHATTERING
EXPERT!

EARTHQUAKE EXPERTS

Scientists who study earth-shattering earthquakes are called seismologists (size-moll-ow-gists). And no, their name's got nothing to do with the size of their brains. Though they'd probably like you to think so. Forget pictures of batty professors in long, white coats snoozing away in dusty laboratories. Seismologists are scientists under pressure. Their tricky task is to work out what makes awesome earthquakes tick. But it isn't as simple as it sounds. Earthquakes are horribly unpredictable. No one knows where and when the next quake will hit. Does this put the stressed-out seismologists off? No way. It just makes them keener than ever to crack on and break new ground.

Could you be a seismologist?

Do you have what it takes to be a seismologist? Would you be able to stand the strain? Try this quick quiz to find out. Better still, try it out on your geography teacher.

1 Are you a whizz at maths? Yes/No

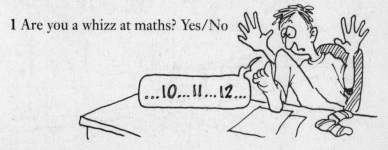

2 Fabulous at physics? Yes/No

3 Marvellous at map-reading? Yes/No

4 Have you got a good imagination? Yes/No

5 Have you got eyes in the back of your head? Yes/No

6 Do you fancy travelling to exotic locations? Yes/No

Answers:

1 You'll need to be. A lot of seismology means collecting scientific information and feeding it into computers. Then working out what on Earth it all means. How do you do this? By doing horribly long and complicated sums, that's how. So you need to be pretty nifty with numbers.

2 Physics is useful for finding out how shock waves travel through the Earth. Unfortunately, shock waves don't go in nice, straight lines. That would be too easy. So plotting their path from A (the earthquake's epicentre) to B (the surface of the ground) isn't nice and straightforward either. As they pass through different types of soil or rock, the wayward waves get reflected back on themselves or bent at an angle (technically speaking, bending's called refraction). Either way, it sends them speeding off in all directions. And guess what? Yep, reflection and refraction are bits of physics.

3 If you get lost finding your way to school (especially if it's geography test day), a map won't help you much. But if you're really serious about seismology, map-reading's a must. I mean, how else will you spot the shock?

4 No, I don't mean imagining things like your teacher telling you you're a genius. That really would be a dream come true. This is the sort of imagination that lets you think up a 3-D picture of what's inside the Earth. Without actually being able to see it. It's essential because this is where earthquakes actually happen. But it's tricky because there aren't any maps. It's a bit like you trying to find that bag of crisps you know you hid under your bed, IN THE DARK.

5 Of course, you don't really need eyes in the back of your head. (Think of the fortune you'd have to spend in cool sunshades!) But you do need to be observant.

So are you on the ball or would you sleep through anything? Try filling in this real-life earthquake questionnaire. It's for finding out how you'd react in an earthquake. Even if you've never lived through a real-life earthquake, think about how you might answer the questions if you had.

EARTHQUAKE QUESTIONNAIRE

1. Where were you when the earthquake happened?
2. What time was the tremor?
3. Did you feel any vibrations?
4. What did you hear?
5. Were you indoors or out?
6. Were you sitting/standing/lying down/active/ sleeping/listening to the radio/watching TV?
7. Were you frightened?
8. Did any doors or windows rattle?
9. Did anything else rattle?
10. Did any hanging objects swing?
11. Did anything fall?
12. Was there any damage?

6 You'll have the chance to visit seismic stations all around the world in such unusual places as the Arctic, the Antarctic, the Himalayas, Africa and New Zealand. Better get your atlas out!

THE WORLD

How do you think you'd do?

Snapshots of the stars

Don't worry if seismology's got you stumped. Sit back and let the real earthquake experts take the strain. Are you ready to rub shoulders with some of the most shockingly clever scientists ever? Here's Sid to introduce you to five real brainboxes…

NAME: John Michell
(1724 – 1793)
NATIONALITY: British

CLAIM TO FAME: Professor of geology at Cambridge University. In 1760 John published the first scientific paper on earthquakes after studying the disastrous Lisbon quake. (The paper was called "Conjectures Concerning the Cause and Observations upon the Phenomena of Earthquakes", in case you were wondering. Unfortunately, it was so horribly boring that not many people bothered to read it.) Still, brainy John was nicknamed the "father of seismology" for his ground-breaking work. He realized that waves travelled at different speeds and worked out a way of finding earthquake epicentres. As if that wasn't enough, in his spare time he was a top astronomer. What a swot.

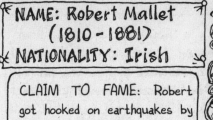

**NAME: Robert Mallet
(1810 - 1881)
NATIONALITY: Irish**

CLAIM TO FAME: Robert got hooked on earthquakes by accident. By training, he was an engineer. He designed railway stations, bridges and lighthouses. All this changed one day, when he read about earthquakes in a book. From then on, Robert became an earthquake bore. Instead of stamps, he collected earthquake books, pamphlets, newspaper articles... You name it, he'd collect it. (He even made his own earthquakes, by exploding gunpowder underground. He had to, you see, because he lived in Ireland, far away from any earthquake zones.) Then he put the whole lot together in a massive book. And that wasn't all. He plotted the biggest earthquakes on a map. And get this. Mallet's map was so amazingly accurate, it's still used today.

**NAME: Andrija Mohorovicic
(1857 - 1936)
NATIONALITY: Croatian**

CLAIM TO FAME: Andrija worked out that earthquakes happen in the Earth's crust. But he found that some of the shock waves shoot through the mantle. The boundary between the crust and mantle was named the Mohorovicic discontinuity, after him.

215

Thankfully, it was such a mouthful, it's now been shortened to Moho. Anyway, Moho was a real clever clogs. Not only was he brilliant at physics and maths, geology and meteorology, he also spoke fluent Croatian, English, French, Italian, Latin, Greek and Czech. So he could say "earthquake" in seven different languages! If he'd wanted to.

NAME: Beno Gutenberg (1889-1960)
NATIONALITY: American

CLAIM TO FAME: Gutenberg spent years studying seismic waves and working out how they travelled. He also helped Charles Richter work out the, er, Richter scale. (So strictly speaking that should have been the Gutenberg-Richter scale.) Again with his pal Richter, Beno showed that three-quarters of earthquakes happen around the shaky Pacific Ocean. But you knew that already. Brainy Beno's best-known books included Earthquakes of North America and The Seismicity of the Earth. OK, I know they sound too boring to read.

NAME: John Milne (1850-1913)
NATIONALITY: British

CLAIM TO FAME: Brilliant John Milne really shook things up by inventing the first practical seismograph (size-mow-graf). That's a posh bit of equipment for measuring earthquakes. Here's the amazing true story of his shocking discovery...

A shocking discovery

John Milne was born in Liverpool, England. He trained at the Royal School of Mines in London and became a mining engineer. (That's someone in charge of building mines underground. Sounds boring – gettit? – but someone had to do it.) When John was just 25 years old, he was offered the job of a lifetime. He became professor of geology and mining at the Imperial College of Engineering in Tokyo, Japan. Posh, or what?

I'LL NEED TO LOOK SMART FOR MY NEW COLLEGE

GET RID OF THE SOCKS!

There was just one teeny little snag... Japan was a very long way from Liverpool and John hated the sea. (Which was strange for someone who loved to travel. As a young man he was always on the move.) Instead he went most of the way overland, through Europe and Russia. It took 11 long, tiring months to reach Japan. And to make matters worse, on John's very first night in his new home, Tokyo was struck by a (small-ish) earthquake! What a shock! And it wouldn't be John's last. As you know, Japan stands on horribly shaky ground. John later wrote that there were earthquakes "for breakfast, dinner, supper and to sleep on". But for the time being, he had other things on his mind. His new job kept him on his toes. Especially the bit where he had to climb to the tops of active volcanoes to inspect their fiery craters. Luckily, the volcanoes didn't blow their tops else daring John would have been a goner. Then who knows what seismologists would have done.

In 1880 a powerful earthquake shook the nearby city of Yokohama. It was enough to make John turn his back on volcanoes and concentrate on earthquakes instead. Immediately, he called a meeting of like-minded scientists and set up the Seismological Society of Japan. (When John put his mind to something, he didn't waste any time you see.) From then on, there was no stopping him. Studying earthquakes became his life's work. But first he needed to find out more about them. The question was how? Then clever John had a brainwave. He needed information and he needed it fast. (And people didn't have telephones or the internet then.) So he sent every post office for miles around a bundle of stamped, self-addressed postcards. All the postmaster (or mistress) had to do was fill in one card every week and post it back to John, describing any tremors. They didn't even need to buy a stamp. Pretty cunning, eh? What's more, it worked! Soon John was swamped with mail bags. There were postcards everywhere. From the answers he got, he was able to draw up detailed maps of every single shock and shudder to shake Japan.

But John still wasn't satisfied. Eyewitness accounts were all very well but you couldn't really rely on them. People were always exaggerating or playing things down. For example, you might accidentally tick the answer "huge" to describe the size of a tremor, when all along you meant "quite small" but you didn't want your postcard to look dead boring. Anyway, what John desperately needed was a posh machine for measuring earthquakes accurately. Various ingenious instruments had been invented but none of them worked very well. Did John give up? Did he, heck. No, he went and invented one of his own. The instrument was called a seismograph (size-mow-graf). It recorded the shock waves from an earthquake so scientists could study and measure them. When an earthquake struck and shook the seismograph, a pin or pen traced the pattern of shaking on to a piece of smoked paper or glass. It was brilliant. Earth-shatteringly brilliant.

Getting the shakes

Basic seismographs haven't changed much since John Milne's time. Which just shows how bloomin' brainy he was. But how on Earth do these marvellous machines work? Do you need to be a genius geographer to use one? Or is it something even your teacher could grasp? Who better to guide you through the muddle than Sid's very own Uncle Stan, the handyman.

MORNIN', STAN HERE. NOW WHAT'S THIS ABOUT SEISMOGRAPHS? PESKY THINGS, I AGREE. NEVER MIND, YOU STICK WITH ME AND WE'LL SOON HAVE THE BEAUTY UP AND RUNNING. FIRST YOU NEED TO GET TO KNOW HOW ALL THE BITS AND PIECES WORK.

Your Seismograph...

frame (fixed to the ground)

spring

heavy weight

squiggly pattern

shaking Earth

rotating roll of paper

scratchy pen

HOW IT WORKS...

WHEN THE GROUND SHAKES, THE FRAME SHAKES TOO, THIS SHAKES THE ROLL OF PAPER, THE WEIGHT DOESN'T MOVE, SO THE PEN FIXED TO IT SCRATCHES A PATTERN ON THE PAPER.

Checking the print-out

The posh technical term for the squiggly lines on the paper is a seismogram (size-mow-gram). Oh they like making things difficult, these scientists. The squiggles show the shock waves from an earthquake. The bigger the squiggles, the bigger the quake. Still with me? Good. Now you've just got to decipher your seismogram, and you're home and dry.

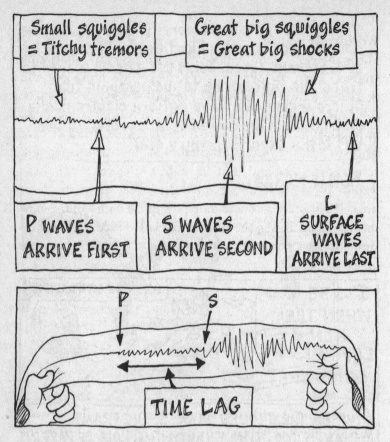

Small squiggles = Titchy tremors

Great big squiggles = Great big shocks

P WAVES ARRIVE FIRST

S WAVES ARRIVE SECOND

L SURFACE WAVES ARRIVE LAST

P   S

TIME LAG

The size of the waves is used to work out the earthquake's magnitude. The closer the earthquake, the bigger the waves.

STAN'S TOP TIP: For more accurate readings, try burying your seismograph underground. I've done that with quite a few of mine. But don't forget to check it regularly. If you can remember where to dig...

Worldwide watch

For many years, John Milne continued his earth-shattering studies. Then in 1895 disaster struck. Fire broke out and destroyed John's home and his precious observatory. Luckily, John and his wife escaped unhurt but his priceless collection of books and instruments went up in smoke. Years of hard work were lost in minutes. Shattered, John left Japan and returned to England, but he didn't stop his earthquake watch. In his new home, on the Isle of Wight, he built himself a brand-new observatory, complete with a brand-new seismograph. It was the first of many. By 1902, he'd set up similar observatories all over the world to keep a 24-hour eye on earthquakes.

Today, the Worldwide Standardized Seismic Network (WSSN, for short) has monitoring stations all over the world, measuring earthquakes as they happen. Using the latest high-tech seismographs, they can pinpoint the epicentre of a major quake in just 15 minutes. And sound the alarm…

Earth-shattering fact

The first ever seismograph was invented in China in about AD 130. It was built by Zhang Heng, a brilliant mathematician, astronomer, map-maker, painter, poet, and, er, seismograph-maker. (Don't some people make you sick?) But it didn't look like any seismograph you'd see today. It was a big bronze vase ringed with bronze dragons and toads. Each dragon held a bronze ball in its mouth. Inside the vase hung a heavy pendulum. When the Earth shook, the pendulum tilted, making the dragon furthest from the earthquake's epicentre drop its ball. Did this convoluted contraption work?

Incredibly, it did!

MAY I HAVE MY BALL BACK, PLEASE?

Teacher teaser

If you're thinking of taking up seismology seriously, you'll need more than a seismograph. Why not baffle your teacher with the names of some other impressive-sounding instruments. Try this one for starters:

PLEASE, MISS, MY CREEPMETER'S ON THE BLINK!

GO AND SEE THE SCHOOL NURSE

What on Earth are you talking about?

I DON'T THINK I SHOULD HAVE PACKED THAT TILTMETER!

If you're itching to get out and get on with your measuring (are you raving mad?), don't go just yet. Your seismograph might be up and running but it can only get the measure of an earthquake AFTER THE EARTHQUAKE'S OVER. It can't tell you where a quake might happen next. So before you go charging off, read the next chapter. Please. It might be a matter of life and death.

SHOCKING WARNING SIGNS

Never mind fancy instruments with fine-sounding names. What if your new-fangled seismograph breaks down under the strain? Then you'd be in serious trouble. Besides, earth-shattering earthquakes are so horribly hard to predict, seismologists need all the extra help they can get. So how on Earth can you tell if and when an earthquake's about to strike? Is it even possible? Could you spot the shocking warning signs?

OOOOOOH! EARTHQUAKE

Could you be a seismologist?

The ground starts shaking and you're scared stiff. You run into the street, just before your house collapses behind you. You've lost everything, your best trainers, your precious collection of computer games. But you're lucky to be alive. If only you'd known to expect an earthquake. Then you could have grabbed your belongings and got out of there, fast. Are there any warning signs you could have looked out for? Take a look at the clues below. Seismologists think they may be tell-tale signs of stress. Tick the box if you see them.

1 Weird water. Weird things happen to water just before earthquakes. For months or even years before, water levels in wells get lower and lower. Then, suddenly, the water shoots back up again. Other watery signs include foaming lakes, boiling seas and fountains that won't stop flowing. See if you notice anything strange next time you have a bath. (Remember the bath? It's that big tub thing in the bathroom?)

2 Gushing geysers. Geysers are gigantic jets of steam and scalding water that's heated to boiling point by hot rocks underground. Then it bursts into the air. You could set your watch by certain geysers. Take Old Faithful in California, USA. It usually erupts every 40 minutes. Regular as clockwork. Except before an earthquake, that is. Then the gap doubles to two hours or more. Scientists aren't sure why this happens but they're not taking any chances. They've got a computer watching this gushing geyser 24 hours a day.

TICK IF YOU'VE SPOTTED

OL' FAITHFUL

EARTHQUAKE WEEKLY

TICK IF YOU'VE SPOTTED

3 Ghastly gases. Radon is a ghastly gas given off by underground rocks. It seeps to the surface in springs and stream water. Before an earthquake, scientists have noticed that the seeping starts to speed up. It seems that stressed-out rocks release more radon. This is exactly what happened just before the 1995 Kobe quake. Unfortunately, the warning signs were ignored.

4 Frightful foreshocks. Before a big quake you often get lots of little mini-quakes. Seismologists call them foreshocks. They get bigger and stronger as the stress builds up. And they're pretty good clues, *if* they happen. Trouble is you sometimes don't feel any foreshocks at all. Not even the tiniest tremble. Or if you do, they may just fizzle out again, without doing any damage.

5 Bright lights. If the sky fills with fireworks (and it's not 5 November yet), watch out. An earthquake might be around the corner. An hour before the Kobe quake, people saw flashes of red, green and blue light streaking across the sky. The tricky technical name for this is fractoluminescence (frakto-loom-in-essence) which means broken lights. Scientists think the lights are caused by smashed-up bits of sparkly quartz, a crusty crystal found in rocks.

6 Stormy weather. For years, people believed in "earthquake weather". Trouble is, they couldn't agree what it was. Some said it was calm weather with clear, blue skies. Others said it was stormy weather with frightening lightning and pouring rain. Who was right? Neither, I'm afraid. You can blame the weather for lots of things, like not being able to go out on your bike. But you can't blame it for earthquakes.

How many warning signs did you spot? Hopefully, you won't have ticked anything. Which means you're perfectly safe and sound, and don't need to worry.

Earth-shattering fact
In October 1989, a seismologist in California detected electrical signals coming from the ground. The signals got stronger and stronger. Then, 12 days later, the earth-shattering Loma Prieta earthquake struck. Were the signals sounding a warning? The shocked scientist certainly thought so. He reckoned the stressed-out rocks had set the signals off. (Note: before you get too excited, guess what? Yep. Other horrible seismologists totally disagree!)

Alarming animals

If you don't think any of these warnings would work, don't worry. Try some old-fashioned folklore instead. Some people say animals start acting oddly before earthquakes. Scientists think animals may be reacting to very high-pitched sounds that we can't hear, coming from tiny cracks around the area that's about to quake. So watch out if your pet cat *stops* chasing mice or your pet dog *starts* purring. You may be in for a nasty shock. Which of the following wildlife warning signs are too way-out to be true?

a) Catfish wriggle and leap out of water. TRUE/FALSE?

b) Rats panic and run away. TRUE/FALSE

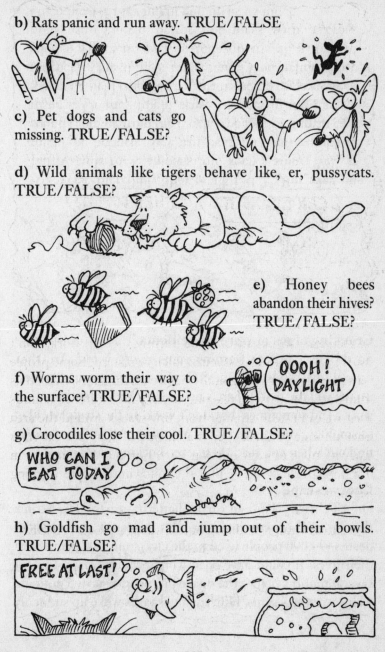

c) Pet dogs and cats go missing. TRUE/FALSE?

d) Wild animals like tigers behave like, er, pussycats. TRUE/FALSE?

e) Honey bees abandon their hives? TRUE/FALSE?

f) Worms worm their way to the surface? TRUE/FALSE?

OOOH! DAYLIGHT

g) Crocodiles lose their cool. TRUE/FALSE?

WHO CAN I EAT TODAY

h) Goldfish go mad and jump out of their bowls. TRUE/FALSE?

FREE AT LAST!

Cracking clues or pure coincidence?

So do any of these warning signs *really* work? Are they crucial quake-busting clues? Or just amazing coincidences? To tell you the truth, there's no easy answer. Sometimes they work. And sometimes they don't work. In the shaky world of seismology, you can't rely on anything. As you're about to find out when you read these two shocking true stories…

Lucky escape

On 4 February 1975 an earth-shattering earthquake struck the city of Haicheng in China. But instead of thousands of deaths (90,000 people lived in the city), only 300 people lost their lives. It could have been worse. Much worse. But for several months before the quake hit, people started noticing weird warnings signs. Hibernating snakes woke up suddenly

232

and slithered sleepily out of their holes, even though it was still winter and they weren't meant to wake up until the spring. Groups of rats were seen running round in circles. What's more, there were 500 foreshocks in the space of three days. It all added up to a massive shock. Fortunately, the authorities decided to take notice of these warning signs. They couldn't predict exactly when an earthquake might strike, but they weren't prepared to take any chances. Finally, at 2 p.m. on 4 February, the city was evacuated. People got ready to spend the freezing night outdoors in tents and straw shelters. Five and a half hours later, at 7.36 p.m., the earthquake struck… It measured 7.3 on the Richter scale. The evacuation had come in the nick of time.

Total disaster

But had the warnings signs done the trick? Could they really be relied on? Many seismologists dismissed the prediction as a fluke. True, thousands of lives had been saved. But it could have been a lucky guess. Were they right? Eighteen months later, at 3.43 a.m. on 28 July 1976, another Chinese city was struck by another awesome earthquake. This quake measured 7.8 on the Richter scale. But the people of

Tangshan weren't so lucky. There were no warning signs whatsoever. No startled snakes. No rattled rats. No rumbling foreshocks. Nothing. In little over a minute, more than 250,000 people were killed. Thousands more were badly injured. The city itself was completely demolished. It was one of the most devastating earthquakes ever. And nobody saw it coming…

Can we really predict earthquakes?

Will earthquakes ever be properly predicted? Can seismologists ever hope to stay one step ahead? Horribly simple questions, you might think. Horribly simple questions … with impossibly tricky answers. So tricky that even the earth-shattering experts can't agree. Just listen to these two, for starters…

No! It's not like forecasting the weather, you know. We can't give nice, precise predictions. I mean, we can't say an earthquake of a certain size will strike a certain place at a certain time. It's not like saying it'll rain in Spain next Tuesday. (Not that weather forecasts are always right.) It simply isn't possible. We just don't know enough about the Earth's insides. Besides, some earthquakes strike without any warning. So there's no way of telling they're even on their way.

Yes! We can give very general warnings. We can say a place can expect a big earthquake sometime this century. But we can't say exactly when or where. It's all down to probability. A bit like you saying you might get round to doing your homework sometime this week. Not horribly exact, is it? But we can pinpoint possible danger zones on a map. So people have time to prepare. OK, it's not much. But it's better than nothing.

If seismologists could even give 20 seconds' (yes, *seconds*) warning, they could save thousands of lives. But scientists have to be careful. A false alarm could be fatal. If they order an evacuation, and no earthquake hits, people might not be so keen to listen next time. Even if they could predict an earthquake, of course, they couldn't do anything to stop it happening. And that's the only thing they know for certain!

SURVIVING THE SHOCK

OK, so your pet cat's left home. DON'T PANIC. Your cat's most likely off chasing mice. It's very, very unlikely that this means an earthquake's about to strike. But you never know. So what would you do if the Earth suddenly shattered? How would you cope? No idea? Luckily Sid's here with his earth-shattering guide to earthquake survival. Don't go to bed without it…

Earth-shattering earthquake survival guide

Hi, Sid here. If you live in a quake zone, it pays to be prepared. Better safe than sorry, I always say. Places used to earth-shattering earthquakes practise regular earthquake drills. They're a bit like the fire drills you have at school, except you don't have to spend hours standing in the playground in the soaking rain. Thank goodness. Anyway, to practise staying safe in an earthquake, here are some essential dos and don'ts:

DO…
- **Stock up on supplies.** Pack an emergency survival kit. You'll need a fire extinguisher, a torch (with spare batteries), a first-aid kit, tinned food (don't forget a tin-opener and food for your cat – he's bound to come home in the end), bottled water (enough for three days), sleeping

bags or blankets, warm clothes and sturdy shoes (for walking over rubble and broken glass). Keep these things somewhere handy and make sure everyone in your family or class knows where they are.

- **Listen to the radio.** Keep a radio (and more spare batteries) in your emergency kit. After the quake, communications may be cut for several days or even weeks. So stay in touch by tuning in to your radio for information and advice.

- **Be prepared.** Make sure everyone in your family or class knows what to do. (Practise beforehand.) Fix up a meeting place for after the quake in case you get split up.

- **Turn off the gas and electricity.** The quake may break gas pipes and snap power lines. So you'll need your torch for seeing in the dark. Never, ever light a match. If there's been a gas leak, everything could go up in flames.

- **Crouch under a sturdy table.** Or under your desk if you're at school. Cover your head with a cushion or pillow, and press your face into your arm. This'll protect your head and eyes from broken glass and flying objects. Hold on tight to the table leg. Now don't move until the shaking stops. Remember, DUCK, COVER AND HOLD ON. (If you're not near a table, stand in a doorway. Doorframes are pretty strong.)

DON'T…
- **Rush outside.** Wait until the house stops shaking before you rush outside. Otherwise you might get hit by flying glass or debris. (Or you might fall out of a window. Remember poor Thomas Chase?) The general rule is: if you're inside, stay inside and if you're outside, stay put.

- **Use the stairs.** If you live in a block of flats, or you're at school, stay away from the stairs. At least until the shaking's stopped. You could easily fall or get crushed. Whatever happens, don't use the lift. If the power's cut, you'll be trapped.

- **Stand by a building.** Once the shaking's stopped and you can go outside, find an open space to stand in. Stay away from buildings, trees, chimneys, power lines, and anything that might fall on top of you.

- **Go for a drive.** At least, not until the shaking's over. If you're in a car, slow down and stop in an open space. But watch out for falling rocks and landslides. And don't go anywhere near a bridge. It'll probably collapse with you on top. Stay inside the car until the shaking's stopped.

- **Use the phone.** For the first few days after the earthquake, don't use the phone. If it's really, really urgent, OK. But don't phone your friends for a chat. It might clog up the phone lines and stop emergency calls getting through.

HELLO, DENTAL SURGERY? I'D LIKE TO CHANGE MY APPOINTMENT...

Earthquake rescue

Phew! You've made it. But you've been lucky. In the chaos that follows a major earthquake, thousands of people may be injured or killed. Many are buried under collapsed buildings, leaving the rescue teams with no time to lose. But it's a horribly risky job. At any moment, a building could come crashing down on top of the rescuers, especially if small aftershocks hit it. Besides, they may only have tools like pick-axes, spades, or even their bare hands to work with. Even with the latest high-tech equipment, like cameras that detect body heat and listening devices, it's a race against time. (Specially trained dogs are also used. Not so high-tech but brilliant at sniffing out survivors.) The rescuers know they have to work fast. Without much air or water, trapped victims may only have days to live. For some people, help arrives too late if it arrives at all. But it isn't all bad news. Sometimes, somehow, against all the odds, miracles do happen. Take the extraordinary events in Mexico City…

EARTH-SHATTERING FACT FILE

DATE: 19 September 1985
LOCATION: Mexico City, Mexico
TIME: 7.18 a.m.
LENGTH OF SHOCK: 3 minutes
MAGNITUDE: 8.1
DEATH TOLL: 10,000
THE SHOCKING FACTS:

• The epicentre was 400 km away, off the coast. It took a minute for the shock waves to reach the city.
• Thirty-six hours later a second massive shock struck. It measured 7.5 on the Richter scale.
• The city centre was hardest hit with thousands of buildings damaged and destroyed.

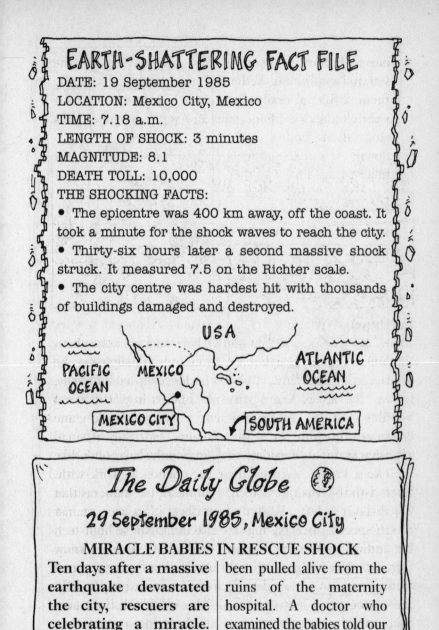

USA

ATLANTIC OCEAN

PACIFIC OCEAN

MEXICO

MEXICO CITY

SOUTH AMERICA

The Daily Globe 🌐

29 September 1985, Mexico City

MIRACLE BABIES IN RESCUE SHOCK

Ten days after a massive earthquake devastated the city, rescuers are celebrating a miracle. Two new-born babies have been pulled alive from the ruins of the maternity hospital. A doctor who examined the babies told our reporter, "It's wonderful news. Babies are pretty tough, you know. When they suffer a really big shock, they're able to slow their bodies right down. It's like animals hibernating. That way, they can stay alive for a surprisingly long time without food or water."

OH, BABY!

The babies had a very lucky escape. The multi-storey hospital in which they were born collapsed like a house of cards. Its twisted remains are all that are left. About a thousand doctors, nurses and patients were buried under the rubble.

TOTAL COLLAPSE

PET RESCUE

It's the same story all over the city. Since the quake struck, exhausted rescuers have worked around the clock to pull survivors out. As the days wear on, their task becomes even grimmer. Now there are mainly dead bodies to bring out. But finding the babies has given the rescuers a much-needed boost. One man told us, with tears in his eyes, "It's like a beacon of hope in all the misery and blackness. We'd almost given up hope of finding anyone else alive. These little ones have given us the strength we needed to carry on with our efforts."

Quake-proof construction

In an earth-shattering earthquake, it's not shock that kills people but collapsing buildings. So what can be done to cut the risk? Well, architects and engineers are already working on the problem. They're trying to build quake-proof buildings that can really stand the strain.

BUILDERS FOR HIRE

HOUSE STARTING TO SWAY?

WALLS STARTING TO CRACK?

NEED QUAKE-PROOFING YOU CAN RELY ON?

LOOK NO FURTHER...

SACKED

RUMBLE, CRUMBLE, TUMBLE & SONS BUILDERS

LET US TAKE THE STRAIN

SMALL PRINT: DON'T BLAME US IF YOUR HOUSE FALLS DOWN. WITH EARTHQUAKES THERE ARE NO GUARANTEES. QUAKE-PROOFING MIGHT DO THE TRICK. THEN AGAIN, IT MIGHT NOT. SORRY.

Want to make sure your house survives the shock and stays standing? But daren't trust the small ads? Why not do it yourself? Sneak a look in this dusty but helpful DIY manual to find out what you need to do. And if you can't tell one end of a hammer from the other, don't worry. Here's Sid's Uncle Stan back to help you with more of his handy hints and tips.

BUILDING FOR BEGINNERS

Lesson 1: Why do buildings fall down?

Before you learn how to keep your house standing up, you need to find out why it might fall down. Are you brave enough to shake your house down?

WHAT YOU NEED:

- A SMALL PLASTIC BOTTLE OF ORANGE SQUASH* (FOR THE HOUSE)

- A PIECE OF CARD (FOR THE EARTH)

WHAT TO DO:

1. PLACE THE BOTTLE ON THE CARD

2. PUSH THE CARD SLOWLY BACKWARDS AND FORWARDS

3. DO THIS AGAIN REALLY QUICKLY THIS TIME

4. DO THIS AGAIN AT A SPEED SOMEWHERE BETWEEN THE TWO

What happens?
a) The bottle shakes a bit but doesn't fall over.
b) The bottle sways but doesn't fall over.
c) The bottle sways a lot and falls over.

Answer: It depends how fast you push the card. If you push slowly, the bottle wobbles a bit but doesn't fall over. If you push quickly, it sways at the top but still stays up. But if you push at a speed somewhere between the two, the bottle falls over. This is because it's shaking at exactly the same frequency** as the card. It's the same when an earthquake strikes. If a building shakes at exactly the same frequency as the ground, it soon topples over.

* You can drink the squash when you've finished this chapter. DIY can be thirsty work. Don't use fizzy pop though. It'll spurt all over the place when you open the bottle and make a terrible mess.

** Frequency's the tricky technical term for the number of shock waves passing through it each second.

STAN'S HANDY HINTS NO. 1

Pick the shape carefully when you're planning your house. Take a look at these two barmy buildings. Which one do you think would work best in an earthquake?

GIVE UP? IN FACT, THEY BOTH WORK BRILLIANTLY. THE PYRAMID SHAPE, ON THE LEFT, IS GREAT IN AN EARTHQUAKE. THIS PARTICULAR BUILDING'S IN SAN FRANCISCO. IN THE 1989 LOMA PRIETA QUAKE, ITS 49 STOREYS SWAYED A BIT BUT DIDN'T FALL DOWN. THE BEEHIVE SHAPE, ON THE RIGHT, IS ANOTHER CRACKING DESIGN. IT'S SHORT AND SQUAT AND KEEPS ITS FEET FIRMLY ON THE GROUND.

LESSON 2: STOPPING THE SHAKING

OK, so now you know why buildings fall down in an earthquake. But how can you keep them standing? The first thing you've got to do is cut down the shaking. If your house doesn't shake so much, it's less likely to tumble. There's a range of techniques you can use. All tried and tested by yours truly. You could…

• **Fit shock absorbers.** Shock absorbers are giant rubber pads used to soak up shock waves. Build them into a wall and you'll cut down the shaking. They've even been used on the Golden Gate Bridge in shaky San Francisco. If another quake strikes, they'll stop the roadway smashing into the towers and bringing the whole lot down. (With any luck.)

• **Make it some sandwiches.** No, not the sort you get filled with cheese or tuna fish. These sandwiches are made from thick layers of rubber and steel. Fancy sinking your chops into one? Fix the sandwiches to your building's foundations. They'll hold it up *and* stop it shaking.

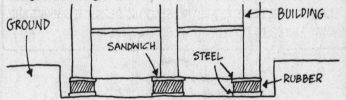

• **Weigh it down.** Some high-rise buildings have heavy weights at the top. You could call them top-heavy, ha! ha! The weights are worked electronically. When a quake hits, they rock in the opposite direction to the shaking. Balancing it out. Brilliant, eh? But horribly expensive. If you're short of cash, they're not for you.

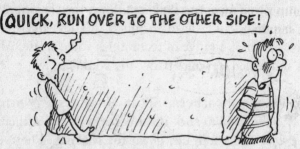

QUICK, RUN OVER TO THE OTHER SIDE!

• **Put up some wallpaper.** That's right, wallpaper. But not the flowery stuff you get at your granny's. This is wallpaper like never before. And your granny would *hate* it. It looks like a roll of shiny black plastic. You paste it on and leave it to dry. Just like ordinary wallpaper. But there's nothing ordinary about this stuff. When it's dry, it's 17 times harder than steel! That's seriously tough stuff. So instead of your wall cracking up, the seismic super-paper holds it all together.

• **Clear out the garage.** If you're thinking of building a garage under your house, think again. Large spaces like garages make the ground floor horribly unstable. If you've already got a garage, clear all the junk out (actually this bit's not essential but your parents will be pleased), then fix the garage to the foundations with giant springs. They'll bend with the shock, then ping back into place once the shaking's over. Leaving your house standing.

OOOPS!

STAN'S HANDY HINTS NO. 2

The best material to build with is something that gives, like wood or reinforced concrete (that's concrete strengthened with steel). Something that'll bend a bit. Don't use brittle bricks or hollow concrete blocks. They'll break if the quake's a big 'un. I'd also use shatter-resistant glass, if I were you.

HOUSE KIT

LESSON 3: TESTING YOUR BUILDING

Right, it's crunch time. You've quake-proofed your house but will it stand up? Until it feels the full force of a real-life earthquake, you can't really tell. But a real-life earthquake's the last thing you want. So what on Earth do you do? Here's what the experts suggest:

1 First, build a model of your house. It doesn't need to be exactly the same size. A scaled-down version will do.

2 Next, find a shake-table. No, a table with a wobbly leg won't do. This is a high-tech bit of equipment for testing out buildings in earthquake conditions. They're horribly expensive so you might need to borrow one from the experts.

3 Place your model on the table. Then make the table shake. (Note: you don't need to do the shaking yourself. A computer will do it for you. They're specially programmed to do just that.)

4 Stand back and watch what happens. If your house falls down, start again. (And this time, make sure you follow all the instructions.) If your house stays up, congratulations. You're obviously a whizz at seismic DIY.

STAN'S HANDY HINTS NO.3

It's a good idea to fix wardrobes and bookcases to the wall, so they don't fall on top of you during an earthquake. Fix latches on your kitchen cupboards. The last thing you want is flying tins of baked beans. If you can't find the fixings you need, try a company called Quake Busters in California. (Yes, it's a real company!) I've heard they'll fix anything.

THAT'LL STOP THE DOG FLYING ABOUT

LESSON 4: CHOOSING YOUR SITE

Be careful where you build your house. Some types of ground are shakier than others. Don't choose a spot where the ground's horribly soggy or soft. You'd be asking for trouble. When this type of soil's shaken up, the water in it rises to the surface, turning the soil to jelly. You won't get a building to stand up in that. I mean, have you ever tried standing a spoon in a bowl of wobbly jelly?

This is what happened to Mexico City in 1985. The city's built on a dried-out lake bed. A very bad move indeed. When the earthquake hit, the lake bed turned to jelly. Some buildings sank straight into the ground. Others tilted over on their sides. To make matters worse, the lake bed's shaped like a bowl. So what, you might ask? Well, the shape made the shock waves bigger and stronger. Which made the damage and devastation many, many times worse.

So what type of ground is best to build on? Somewhere nice and rock-solid would do.

STAN'S HANDY HINTS NO. 4...

Make sure you follow the local building code. Most quake-prone cities have one. Trouble is, quake-proofing's a seriously costly business. And some builders cut costs by breaking the rules. Instead of proper materials, they'll use cheaper, shoddier stuff, turning their buildings into killers. Besides, in poor countries, many people can't afford to live in posh, quake-proofed buildings. So they end up living in death-traps instead. It's a very tricky problem.

Shocking, isn't it? But it isn't all doom and gloom. All over the world, seismologists, architects and engineers are working hard to make shaky cities safer. Will they succeed? Who knows? The only way they can really put their new buildings to the test is to wait for the next earthquake...

A SHAKY FUTURE?

So is the future set to get shakier? Or will earthquakes soon be a thing of the past? Let's go back to our stressed-out seismologists and see what they have to say. Oh, dear, they're *still* squabbling…

> If you think things have got off to a shaky start, watch out! They're set to get even shakier. The Big One could strike at any time. And, believe me, it'll be a megaquake. Where will it strike? Hard to tell. Chances are it'll be along a fault. A fault that's been nice and quiet for centuries. A fault where the strain's been building up and up, until suddenly it reaches breaking point. The Big One's already long overdue. Help! Help! Is there a table I can hide under?

Don't listen, it may never happen. Earthquakes aren't any more frequent than they used to be. It's just that more of them hit the headlines. And we scientists have got more sensitive seismographs so we can spot the small ones more easily. It might be ages before we can predict earthquakes accurately. If we ever can. But we're finding out lots more about them. So, even if we can't beat them just yet, we can learn to live with them. Pssst! You can come out from under the table now!

So you see, even the experts don't know for certain. But don't go digging up the playground just yet to see if *your* school's on shaky ground. (It *won't* get you out of double geography. Shame on you!) It's more likely your teacher will come down on you like a tonne of bricks for reading this book in class than you'll be shaken up by an earthquake. Of course with earthquakes you never know what shocks are in store, do you? You'll just have to wait and see. And that, I'm afraid, is the earth-shattering truth!

If you're still interested in finding out more, here are some seismic websites to visit:

http://www.iris.edu
The Incorporated Research Institutes for Seismology. With posters, web pages, maps and photos.

http://www.gsrg.nmh.ac.uk
The British Geological Survey's website, with up-to-date lists and maps of UK earthquakes.

http://www.earthquake.usgs.gov
The US Geological Survey. Maps, lists, facts and figures of earthquakes in the USA and around the world.

http://www.earthquakes.com
The Global Earthquake Response Center is an American site full of reports and information on earthquakes from around the world.

http://tlc.discovery.com/tlcpages/greatquakes/greatquakes.html
Check out the earthquake simulator and learn about the worst earthquakes this century.